THE MILIT... ON ENGLISH WATERWAYS 1798–1844

By
HUGH J. COMPTON
and
ANTONY M. CARR-GOMM

with 21 illustrations and 10 maps

RAILWAY & CANAL HISTORICAL SOCIETY

First published in 1991
by the Railway & Canal Historical Society
Registered office: Fron Fawnog, Hafod Road, Gwernymynydd, Mold, Clwyd CH7 5JS
Registered charity no.256047

ISBN 0 901461 14 8

Designed and typeset by
Malcolm Preskett and Carol Davie
Printed in England by
Hobbs the Printers of Southampton

FRONT COVER
Royal Waggon Train on the Royal Military Canal
(see illustration no.26)

BACK COVER
The Royal Military Canal at Hythe
(see illustration no.28)

INSIDE COVERS
Reproductions of marching orders
(back cover courtesy of Regimental Headquarters,
Coldstream Guards)

THE MILITARY
ON ENGLISH WATERWAYS
1798–1844

THIS BOOK IS DEDICATED TO
those men of the armed forces who travelled both by
day and night in all weather conditions; and to our
wives who made the telling of this story possible

Paddington Basin in 1813 on the Grand Junction Canal.

This was the place to which soldiers together with their wives and children trudged when they wanted to board a fly-boat from London.

Contents

Illustrations, Maps and Plans

Foreword

From earliest times until the end of the eighteenth century the quickest way in which any army could move overland was on its feet. But in 1798 Britain initiated a new method of travel by using barges on canals; they thus effectively halved the time it took to move troops from one place to another within England.

The country was at that time faced with the possibility of an invasion by Napoleon, and many troops had to be moved to the South Coast and elsewhere. This led the Government to consider using the existing network of canals for this purpose, and it was soon found that they provided a means of transport for men and stores that was not only quicker but also easier and cheaper than marching. For the next four decades England's canals were widely used for troop movements, with the skilled assistance of that well-known firm of carriers, Pickford.

The main use initially was defence of the island against invasion by France, and to this end a completely new waterway, the Royal Military Canal, was built in Kent and Sussex from 1804 to 1806. At the same time the canals between London and Liverpool were used to send troops to Ireland, reducing the time taken to reach Liverpool from fourteen days to four or five days. An Ordnance Depot was also set up at Weedon in Northamptonshire (where it remains today), and supplies from there were despatched by barge around the country.

With the defeat of France in 1815, the Army continued to use the canals for a wide variety of purposes. A Guards battalion moved from London to Liverpool every year by canal from 1821 to 1827, and there embarked for ceremonial duties in Dublin. In 1826 troops were rushed to Manchester by canal to deal with riots, and by travelling day and night they halved the time it would have taken to march there. In 1838 two Guards battalions were sent to fight in Canada, and a canal barge carried some of their stores from London to Portsmouth.

But the railways had been spreading across England since 1826 and they proved both faster and cheaper than the canals, taking only hours from London to Manchester, for example, instead of days by barge. Finally, it was decided in 1839 that the canals would no longer be used for troop movements, and it was the end of an era.

Hugh Compton and Antony Carr-Gomm have thoroughly researched this most interesting subject, and have produced a highly readable account of the 46 years from 1798 to 1844, when England's canals were extensively used for military transport, before the advent of steam so accelerated the whole pace of war on land and sea, and indeed changed the pace of life. It is rare to find such an original and intriguing piece of history, and the authors have certainly done it justice.

Lieutenant-Colonel Sir Julian Paget Bt CVO
Editor, The Guards Magazine

Introduction

THE excellent canal histories now available contain only brief references to the conveyance of troops on inland waterways, but give no idea of whether this was only a rare occurrence or a quite widely used military procedure.

If we turn to the many published regimental histories covering the Napoleonic period we find that they are largely concerned with battles and scarcely ever comment upon the means by which large bodies of troops moved around this country.

This unresolved question prompted the research which is embodied in the following work. We find that the dictum attributed to the great adversary, 'An army marches on its stomach', is unquestionable. An important alternative to foot-slogging was available on certain well-trodden routes; it involved nothing more arduous than sitting in a canal boat, and was widely used during four decades.

Early in the last century this nation enjoyed a complicated system for the management of the army. Prior to the first tentative reforms of 1837 there were ten or eleven major departments involved. As one modern historian has confirmed, 'The gentlemen of the War Department led an administrative life of exquisite confusion'.

The Secretary of State for the Home Department was in charge of militia, yeomanry and volunteers, and also, later, the new police. With him, usually in the Cabinet, was the Secretary of State for War and Colonies responsible for overall armed forces policy and strategy.

The Commander-in-Chief presided over three departments: there were his Military Secretary and his Adjutant-General overseeing recruiting, discipline, armaments and clothing (but not greatcoats). Then, his Quartermaster General (after 1811 known as Quartermaster-in-Chief) carried out duties which were later those of the general staff. In fact before the Peninsular Campaign drew to a close, the Quartermaster-General, General George Murray, became Wellington's Chief of Staff.

Throughout almost the whole of the years of our studies, this post was held by Frederick Augustus, Duke of York and Albany. The second son of King George III, he presided at Horse Guards from 3 April 1797 for 32 years except for a two-year break near the middle of this period.

The Commander-in-Chief's responsibilities did indeed include the discipline of the cavalry and the infantry, but not that of the Engineers and the Artillery, and as representative of the sovereign he held command of the whole army at home. However, the Duke of Wellington in 1837 had to admit that 'the Commander-in-Chief cannot move a corporal's guard from London to Windsor without going to the civil department for authority – he must get a route'.

In short, the professional soldier of the Hanoverian monarchs was content to distance himself from the Army's civil and financial concerns. Parliament placed these matters in the hands of one of its members, the Secretary at War. In premises that became known as the War Office, he shared the Horse Guards building in Whitehall with the Commander-in-Chief. In 1812 Lord Palmerston, who held this appointment for eighteen years, set out his duties in a definitive memorandum which included the following:

...finance of the Army (and) those matters in which soldiers come into contact with the civil inhabitants of the country, such as quartering, billeting and marching of troops, require the sanction and authority of the Secretary at War.

Alas, these matters were not that simple! This statement took no account of three more senior functionaries. The Master-General of the Ordnance was usually a serving officer and occasionally of Cabinet rank. He was in command of only a small 'Scientific Corps' of Engineers and Artillery. He presided over the supply of ammunition (including the Navy): stores; dealings with landowners; United Kingdom survey and Defensive Works which included fortifications; and also barracks and greatcoats. For all these he prepared his own estimates for parliamentary approval.

Lastly, two officers represented 'the Expending Departments of the Treasury'. The Paymaster-General certainly carried out the duties of the Army's banker, but like the Secretary at War he was also a Member of Parliament: evidence of the Commons' continuing concern over the control of the Army's finances.

Also owing allegiance to the Treasury were the Commissariat officers: they were civil servants but they held double appointments from the War Office. Palmerston gave them general directions as to pay and allowances but they were directly charged with supply of provisions – principally fuel, forage and light – as well as furnishing the troops with land and inland water transport as necessary.

Indeed in our view, just as these various office-holders shared the duties of the day-to-day management of the Army, so did they share in the Army's involvement with canal transport. It was the Secretary at War, together with the Home Secretary, who initiated the marching orders, and when these called for movement by canal the Commissariat officers made all the detailed arrangements

ACKNOWLEDGMENTS

We are most grateful to all those who have helped us in the various stages towards the completion of this work. Writing this book has involved the co-authors in visiting numerous repositories including the Public Record Office at Kew, the British Library and Guildhall Library in London, the County Record Offices at Lewes, London, Maidstone and Warwick plus the National Army Museum at Chelsea and various regimental museums including the archives held by the various Guards regimental headquarters in Wellington Barracks, London; all of whom most willingly made their various records available for inspection. We are grateful to Brigadier Andrew Mayes, Charles Hadfield, Alan Faulkner and Humphrey Household, who have read parts of the original manuscript. Our thanks are due to the following for permission to reproduce photographs and other illustrations: Bill Minns Water-colours of Farnham, frontispiece; National Portrait Gallery of London, Figs 2 and 13; Victoria Gallery of Bath, Fig 3; Broadlands (Romsey)Ltd, Fig 14; National Buildings Record of London, Fig 10; Railway & Canal Historical Society, Figs 5, 7, 17, 20 and 29; Winsor & Newton, Figs 6 and 16; Public Record Office Kew, Fig 21; Author (H.J.Compton) collection, Fig 26; Town and Cinque Port of Hythe, Figs 25, 27 and 28; Brigadier G.E. Dennison OBE, Secretary to the RAOG, Fig 30; Royal Engineer's Library Chatham, Fig 24; S.G.P.Ward MA BLitt, Fig 23. With regard to Maps we are indebted to the Archivist at Warwick, the Estates Officer (South) of British Waterways and others whose outline plans enabled Cartographics of Stoke-on-Trent to produce all the maps in this book.

CHAPTER ONE

Early days

EARLY in 1798 the British Government was evidently in great apprehension of an imminent French landing, and the possibility of them not only landing but overrunning the country, for we find an Act passed, 'for applying in the most expeditious manner, and with the greatest effect, the voluntary services of the King's loyal subjects for the defence of the Kingdom'.

The Lord-Lieutenant of each county was directed to procure returns of the numbers of men residing within the several counties who were available, and we see how this was done in Warwickshire, by an order published in *Aris's Gazette* early in May of that year.

'To the Constable, Tythingman, Headborough, or other Officer of Birmingham, in the Hundred of Hemingford, in the County of Warwick. By Virtue of an Order from the Lord-Lieutenant of the said County unto me directed, you are hereby required to return to his Majesty's Deputy Lieutenant and Justices of the Peace of the said County, at the Sub-division Meeting for the Hundred afore-said, to be held at the Swan Hotel, in Birmingham, in the Hundred and County afore-said, on Tuesday, the Twenty-second Day of May instant, at Ten of the Clock in the forenoon, fair and true Lists, in Writing, of the names of all the men residing within your respective Parish, Tything, or Place, who are of the age of 15 years and under the age of 60 years, distinguishing which of them are, by Reason of Infirmity, incapable of active Service, and which of them are engaged in any Volunteer Corps, and what Corps, and which of them are willing to engage themselves to be armed, arrayed, trayned, and exercised for the Defence of the Kingdom, and upon what terms; and which of them are willing to engage, in cases of Emergency, either gratuitously, or for hire, as Boatmen, or Bargemen, or as Drivers of Carriages or Horses, or Drivers of Waggons or Carts, which may be necessary for the Public Service; and also distinguishing which of them (if any) are Aliens or Quakers, and also to make a Return of all Barges, Boats, Waggons, Carts, and Horses, for riding or drawing, within your respective Parish, Tything, or Place, and which of such Barges, Boats, Waggons, Carts, and Horses, the owners thereof are willing to furnish in cases of Emergency for the Public Service, either gratuitously or for hire; and with what number of Boatmen, Bargemen, Drivers, and other necessary Attendance, and upon what Terms and Conditions, and also a Return of all Gamekeepers and Persons skilful in the use of Fowling Pieces, residing within your Parish, Tything, or Place distinguishing which of them are willing to engage themselves in case an Enemy should have actually landed, to act as Sharpshooters or Rifle-men, and for that Purpose to be formed into a separate Corps, under proper Officers, but not to be called forth except in case of actual Invasion, and then only within the Military District to which the County of Warwick belongs; and also a return of arms they may now possess, specifying also whether it is their wish to receive a Rifle from the Government, and you, the said Constable, Tythingman, Headborough, or other Officer, are to attend at the Day and Place above appointed for the said Meeting, to Verify your Return upon Oath. Given under my hand, the second day of May, 1798.

JAMES GREEN
High Constable'

In this connection it is interesting to note that in the Grand Junction Canal Company's Act for 1793, which authorised the construction of the canal from Braunston in Northamptonshire on the Oxford Canal to Brentford, Middlesex, on

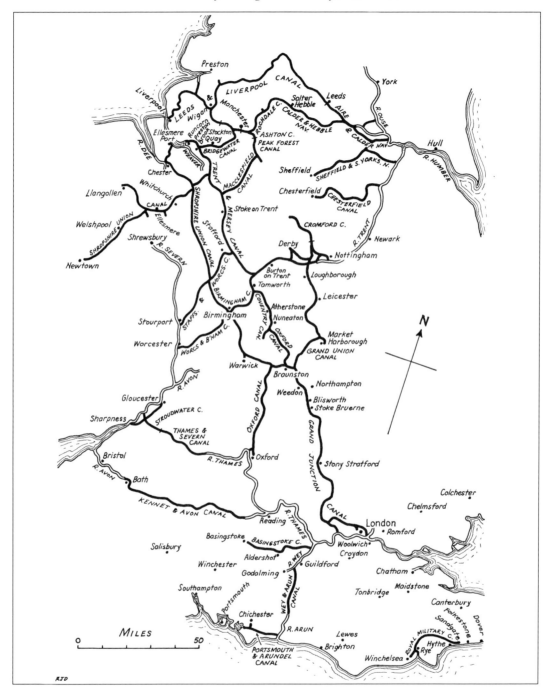

1. The English canal system

2. HRH Frederick August, Duke of York, Field Marshal and for 30 years Commander-in-Chief, d.1827. By his efforts the administration of the army was greatly improved.

the river Thames, there was a clause which read:

'That none of the rates thereby made payable, shall be demanded or taken by virtue of this said Act, for or in respect of any Officers or Soldiers upon their March, or any horses, Arms, or baggage or belonging to such Officers or Soldiers.' [1]

Within five years 17½ miles of the canal had been completed southwards through Braunston tunnel to a wharf at Blisworth in Northamptonshire just to the north of Blisworth tunnel, which was still under construction. Pickfords, the canal carriers, had a depot here from which the Grand Junction Canal Company constructed a 3½ mile long road to connect the wharf with the Northampton – Old Stratford turnpike road.[2]

REINFORCEMENTS FOR IRELAND 1798

Across the water in Ireland there were a number of disturbances which prompted the Government in London early in June 1798, to increase the number of troops stationed there. The main task of carrying out this decision fell upon the Commissary General for Great Britain, Sir Brook Watson. He had led a very varied life which included having his leg bitten off whilst bathing at Havana, Cuba.

Firstly, on 16 June he issued instructions from his office at 10 Parliament Street, London, to his officer in the Eastern District that the Buckinghamshire and Warwickshire militias in camp at Chelmsford were to proceed to Blisworth in Northamptonshire and there board canal boats for Liverpool.[3] The Duke of York, the Commander-in-Chief, had decreed that in view of the extreme urgency the soldiers could travel in waggons to Blisworth. On the same day the Deputy Commissary General, Henry L. Hunter, was instructed to go immediately to

3. Sir Brook Watson (1735–1807) who was appointed in 1798 as Commissary General to the forces in England. He established the detailed procedure for provisioning troops travelling by canal.

Blisworth and hire at least 15 boats for each regiment, which were to be properly washed out and fitted with three rows of rough planks running down the length of each boat, designed as seating for 100 soldiers. Two horses were to be provided for each boat on each stage of the journey to Runcorn, where 'Hoys' took the troops down the Mersey to Liverpool.

General Hunter was to travel with the boats and pay all bills for which he had been advanced £100, and where difficulties arose he was to seek assistance of the local magistrates. On completion of the move, he was to return to London with a full report which he was to present no later than 5 July. No doubt his salary of £1 per day, plus expenses of £1 0s 5d per week were of sufficient reward for this unusual task he was undertaking.

The Grand Junction Canal Company, having been advised of this move, arranged for their Engineer, James Barnes, to be in attendance at Blisworth, together with his assistant, W. Constable, when the regiments were embarking and render such assistance as necessary. Barnes was well qualified for this task, since he had been resident engineer to the Oxford Canal Company over whose northern section between Braunston and Hawkesbury the troops would first be travelling after leaving the Grand Junction Canal. Therefore he was in a good position to advise the military as to problems likely to be encountered on the early stages of their journey, as well as having experience of dealing with the many boatmen whose craft would need to be hired for the journey through to Cheshire.

The clerks to the other companies concerned, viz. Oxford, Coventry and Trent & Mersey Canals, were all advised within the next two days and requested to ensure that their staff gave absolute priority to the passage of the narrow boats when passing through locks or tunnels.

The advice of the impending move as received by the Officer Commanding at Liverpool, Lt General Grinfield, stated that the journey by canal boat was expected to take three days and in the meanwhile he was to ascertain quickly what arrangements could be made for the movement of 'Hoys' to Liverpool from Runcorn, as His Royal Highness, the

Commander-in-Chief, was most anxious that the move be made with the utmost expedition. Among the staff assisting with the arrangements, was Deputy Quartermaster-General Colonel Robert Anstruther, who was instructed to proceed 'post-haste' to Blisworth.

First to move were the 950 men of the Buckinghamshire militia under George Grenville, Marquis of Buckingham, on 20 June 1798 and after an overnight stop at Northampton they reached the village of Blisworth early on the morning of the 22nd.[4] In the event it was found that 18 boats were necessary for their use, since there was also a quantity of baggage as well as 40 artillery men with their two 12-pounder field guns.[5] The Marquis travelled in the last boat which had been specially provided with a small cabin for his personal use. The unit reached Dublin in July and after an uneventful stay, returned to England in May 1799.

One day later came the 900 men of the Warwickshire militia under the Marquis of Hertford, assisted by Lt Col. Packwood and Major Henry Seymour, in 22 narrow boats. Everybody seemed to be aware that the militia units were coming by boat on their way to quell the disturbances in Ireland. Great was the rejoicing, church bells rang out and flags were flown from tall buildings. People congregated at bridges to cheer them on their way and at locks food and drink was provided gratuitously. [6]

Affairs in Ireland, however, were getting even worse, so much so that at one time it was feared that even Dublin would fall to the insurgents, but they were defeated at Vinegar Hill, near Wexford, by troops under General Lake. On 22 August, a French force of 1,100 men landed at Killala Bay and soon took a large part of the County of Mayo. The first troops sent against them at Castlebar ran away so fast that the affair is known as 'the race of Castlebar'. The Government soon decided that further reinforcements were necessary, and on 1 September King George III agreed that in view of the extreme gravity of the situation the Duke of York should order military units to proceed to Ireland as soon as possible, and where necessary inland navigation was to be used (*see table 1*)

However, when the routing instructions were

TABLE 1: *Units ordered to Ireland by the Duke of York in September 1799*

MILITIA REGIMENT	NUMBER OF MEN
Bedfordshire	702
East Suffolk	1073
Herefordshire	1049
Leicestershire	1285
South Lincolnshire	771
West Kent	1086
West Suffolk	1125
Worcestershire	986
Total	8077

worked out and issued, the actual number to travel by canal had been greatly diminished. To start with the 1,049 men of the Herefordshire militia set out by waggon from Brentwood for Blisworth on 3 September. Some were to finish their canal journey at Northwich in Cheshire and others at Middlewich on the Trent and Mersey Canal where they were to await instructions for onward movement to Runcorn. Two days later the 1,086 men of the West Kent militia were instructed to march from Canterbury over the same route and by the same arrangements to Blisworth under Major General Graham.[8] Once again Deputy Commissary General H.L. Hunter had to leave his desk in London, proceed immediately to Blisworth and perform similar duties as before in liaison with W. Constable of the Grand Junction Canal Company. On this occasion Blisworth was not to be the only point at which troops were to embark on canal boats; Nuneaton on the Coventry Canal was also to be included.

On 7 September, the remaining 200 men of the Buckinghamshire militia were to march from Chelmsford and board canal boats on 12 September at Nuneaton in Warwickshire for Middlewich. Also on the same date came 200 men of the Leicestershire militia, under Major General Loftus from Leicester, who embarked on canal boats on the next day, 13 September, for Northwich. The major part of this regiment marched throughout by road.

The press of boats going north must have put a considerable strain on the canal system and

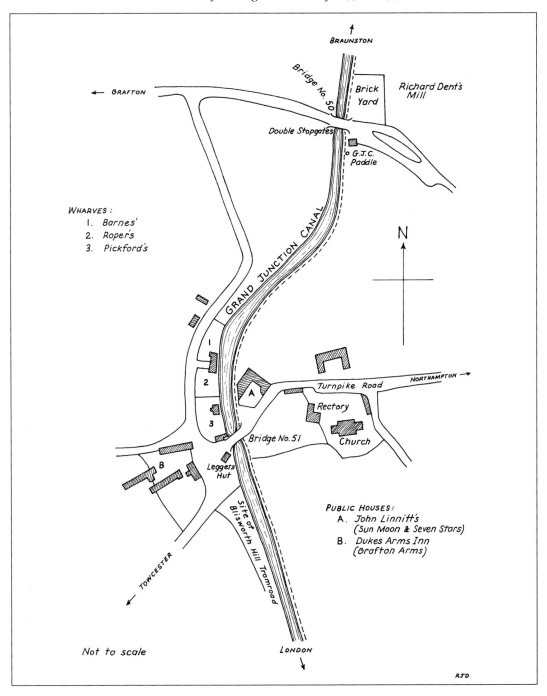

4. Blisworth, on the Grand Junction Canal in Northamptonshire, 1809.

5. Blisworth in 1990. Pickford's wharf on the Grand Junction Canal near the garrison town of Northampton. From here the first military move by canal took place in 1798 and on many occasions thereafter.

severely disorganised the carrying trade. However, the inn keepers alongside the canals traversed must have had a windfall as each man was paid 1½d each day for small beer (about one gallon of a weak brew).

On the face of it therefore, all seems to have gone well as far as the army was concerned, but some of the canal companies were distinctly unhappy. Dunsford, the clerk to the Oxford Canal Company, wrote to Brook Watson on 6 July, claiming £24 5s 4d in respect of the Buckinghamshire militia and £18 5s 3d for the Warwickshire militia.[9] It is interesting to note that according to the canal clerk's records, the former boats weighed on average 23 tons more than the latter – was the artillery responsible for this higher figure? The letter was duly passed to General Hunter, who was responsible for the payment, and in reply he stated he was unaware that the Oxford Company could claim any payment for use of their canal when conveying troops. Dunsford, however, on 13 July sent him copies of their Acts pointing out that there were no clauses in any of them which allowed the army to pass free of tolls. The Trent & Mersey Canal Company made a charge of £200 based on 3,600 men being conveyed, when in fact just over 1,800 had passed.[10]

Following contact with the Marquis of Buckingham, it was ascertained that he had agreed the tolls charged by the Oxford Canal Company and in consequence their bill was paid for his militia's move. Shortly afterwards the company submitted a bill for £39 2s 3d in respect of the movement of the West Kent militia[11] and as this had been compiled on the same basis as that for the Buckinghamshire militia, it was promptly paid.

The original Trent & Mersey Canal Company's bill was found to have been worked out on the basis that each boat weighed 12 tons when conveying 100 troops. The Commissariat objected to this somewhat unusual method of charging and so the Trent & Mersey Company, on reflection, reduced the figure per boat to 6 tons, but added a charge of £58 in respect of the 58 locks passed, thus making the new total £158, which was paid.[12] The clerk to the Coventry Canal Company was a lot more cautious, as he wrote to his counterpart on the Oxford Canal, who on 15 October gave him advice as to how to proceed in the matter.

The only other matter to be cleared up by the Commissariat was a letter from Lt Colonel George Finch-Hatton, a company commander in the West Kent militia, who had complained to the Commander-in-Chief, the Duke of York, that the Commissariat's representative (General Hunter) at Blisworth had not taken any notice of his complaint concerning the accommodation provided for his troops. Enquiries were made, but no further action appears to have been taken in the matter.

Towards the end of this eventful year for canal conveyance of troops, a General Order was issued to Magistrates and Justices of the Peace on 3 December, that they were to impress waggons for the conveyance of stores and baggage belonging to the West Suffolk and South Lincolnshire militias for transport to the canal wharf at Blisworth on the Grand Junction Canal.[13] The units were to march throughout by road to Liverpool, leaving only a small escort to accompany their stores and baggage on the canal boats. Ten days later, followed the stores and baggage of the West Kent and Herefordshire militias, again with a small escort, on the canal boats.

MUTINY ACT 1799

The War Office and the Treasury had obviously learnt their lessons from these moves for by now they were only too well aware that the 1798 Defence of the Realm Act had certain deficiencies. The Grand Junction Canal Act of 1793 however, had certain benefits, not found in any other canal company's Act. So when putting together the next Mutiny Act several interesting clauses concerning troop movement were included in the Bill, which became law on 21 March 1799. Firstly the Secretary at War was to signify when an emergency existed and then the War Office could instruct Magistrates and Justices of the Peace to impress boats, barges, etc. In these special circumstances the canal companies would not be able to charge tolls, but the carrier's charges for provision of crew and horses, etc. were to be paid for by the county in which the magistrate or justice of the peace resided. Furthermore the boats could be used for the conveyance of men, women and children, as well as stores and baggage belonging to soldiers and officers of the regiment.[14]

ROYAL STAFF CORPS GOES TO IRELAND 1803

In 1803, it was decided to impose the means for transmitting messages across Ireland with the erection of alarm beacons and signal forts, the work to be carried out by the Royal Staff Corps, a little known unit of the British Army, which had been founded in 1799 by the Duke of York. A detachment under Captain Robert Henry Sturgeon left Greenwich on 31 October and marched via Barnet, St Albans, Dunstable, Fenny Stratford to Towcester on the Holyhead road (A5).[15] The composition of this 55-man detachment is of special interest as it gives some idea of their skills:

> Capt Richard Henry Sturgeon
> Lt Andrew Long
> Ensign James H. Colleton
> 2 Sgts – Overseers
> 2 Cpls – Blacksmiths
> 1 Drummer
> 14 Carpenters
> 4 Shipwrights/Boat Builders
> 4 Stone Masons
> 2 Bricklayers
> 4 Quarrymen
> 17 Labourers with hedging and ditching
>   qualifications.[16]

Their captain was the sixth senior officer in the Corps and therefore was known to the Commander-in-Chief. Prior to his appointment as Captain on 25 June 1803, he had been in the Artillery. He later served with distinction, being killed in action on 19 March 1814.

6. Stockton Quay *c.*1910 on the Bridgewater Canal. The nearest point to the river Mersey and Liverpool being adjacent to London Bridge, on the road leading to Warrington.

Whilst he was making his way up the Holyhead road, the Commander-in-Chief had issued a directive to the Commissariat General, via the Quartermaster General (Major General Robert Brownrigg) that the detachment was to proceed by canal as from Braunston. Accordingly, Sir Brook Watson saw James Pickford and agreed with him that he would pay £14 for the journey to Stockton Quay.[17] At Towcester in Northamptonshire, 60 miles from London, they received orders to march on to Braunston, 15 miles away, where on 7 November they were to embark on narrow boats. On arrival at Stockton Quay, they were to proceed by the shortest and most convenient route to Liverpool where they were to board a vessel as provided by the Transport service.

After marching down the then long steep 1 in 14 road into Braunston and turning into the wharf, they were disappointed to find that they were not to have exclusive use of a boat, but had to make do with sitting on bales of cotton in the normal 'fly-boat' operated by Pickfords.

However Captain Sturgeon was not the sort of man to overlook these shortcomings in the arrangements, so he wrote a letter of complaint to the Duke of York which resulted in a strong letter of complaint to the carrier. The Trent & Mersey Canal Company, on the other hand, did what they could to speed their passage through the Harecastle tunnel in Staffordshire, whose passage normally took two hours. Because it was built with only just sufficient width to pass one narrow boat, it was the normal practice for boats going north to enter the tunnel in the morning, with those requiring to go southbound having to wait till the afternoon. Their eventful journey to Ireland finally finished when they reached Dublin on 19 November – 20 days after leaving Greenwich.

EMERGENCY ARRANGEMENTS FOR SUPPLY OF BOATS 1803–4

In July 1803 Pickfords wrote to the Duke of York putting at his disposal the whole of their operations to be used as the Government thought fit in the event of an invasion actually taking place, for conveying troops, stores, ammunition, etc. The offer covered 400 horses and 28 boats. They pointed out that a pair of narrow boats left Manchester and London, Paddington each day. Each boat weighed 7½ tons empty, and normally carried up to 15 tons of traffic. To enable the boats to be used at short

notice their wharfingers would be empowered to act on a written order issued by the Officer Commanding in the district from which the movement would commence, and to this end they enclosed a list of their wharfingers:[18]

Paddington – William Wright
Stoke Bruerne – William Horsefall
Braunston – Samuel Lea
Coventry – Thomas Shaw
Derby – James Oaks
Liverpool Duke's Dock – Johnathon Barber
Manchester – James Poulson
Preston Brook – Robert Brerton

One thing they forgot to mention or carefully omitted, was the fact that Blisworth tunnel on the Grand Junction Canal had still not been completed, but to assist traders the canal company had laid a temporary tramway over the

7. Braunston on the Oxford Canal, 1926. The great transhipment depot for fly-boats operating through the east Midlands.

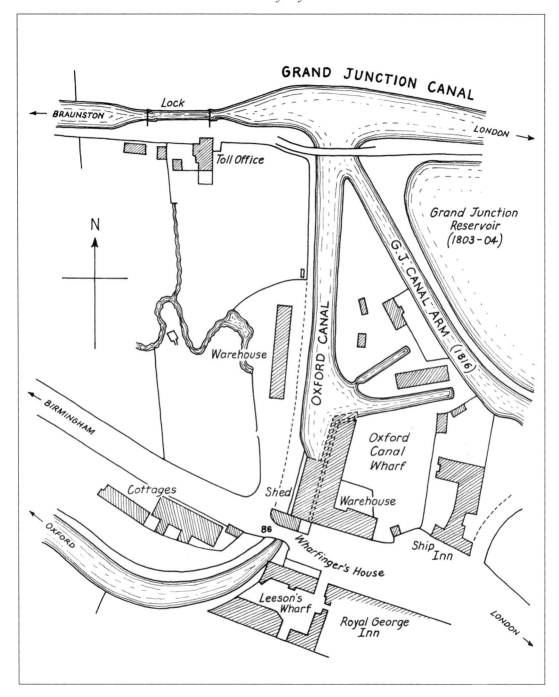

8. The Oxford Canal, where it meets the Grand Junction Canal at Braunston, Northamptonshire, 1835.

hill between the wharfs at Blisworth and Stoke Bruerne.

Similarly in November, the Trent & Mersey Canal Company offered 40 narrow boats to be used on the same basis as those offered by Pickfords.[19] So that Sir Brook Watson could have a complete picture of the boats likely to be available, he arranged in 1804 for the Trent & Mersey Canal Company to supply him with the following details:

(a) Boats employed on the canals between Blisworth and Liverpool.

(b) Minimum time required to assemble 100 boats at any point.

(c) Place-to-place timings based on boats working continuously, throughout the night as well as by day, assuming that horses are readily available at each changeover point.[20]

Next, he turned his attention to the routes from the Thames in London to the river Severn. For this information he wrote to Zachary Allnut, secretary to the Thames Commissioners at Henley, in Oxfordshire, whose governing body comprised 600 elected persons who were responsible for the Thames above Staines. In his letter, dated 18 August, he requested not only details of all barges navigating the Thames, stating name of owner together with residence, but also time required for navigating between the undermentioned places with day and night working and horses being available at changeover points without delay:

    Gloucester – Cirencester
    Cirencester – Lechlade
    Framilode – Stroud
    Stroud – Lechlade
    Lechlade – Oxford
    Oxford – Henley
    Banbury – Oxford
    Bath – Trowbridge
    Trowbridge – Newbury
    Newbury – Reading

Sir Brook Watson next turned his thoughts to the capabilities of other parts of the canal system. This time, on 8 December, he wrote to the Officer Commanding at York requesting details of boats navigating throughout the waterways of the West Riding of Yorkshire.[21]

REGIMENTAL JOURNEYS TO MERSEYSIDE 1804

On 16 December 1803 marching orders were issued by the Commissariat for 88 officers and 1,940 other ranks of 1st and 2nd Battalions of the 30th Regiment of Foot (East Lancashire) to proceed from Ipswich to Braunston in four divisions spread over 21 to 24 December inclusive.[22] Some Christmas – marching across England! James Pickford was sent details on 19 December and two days later was requested to call upon Sir Brook Watson to discuss the detailed arrangements. It was then agreed that 40 boats were to be supplied with folded seats and covered accommodation as recommended by Sturgeon of the Royal Staff Corps. This was quite important as women and children were also to be conveyed. As embarkation would be taking place over the period 30 December to 3 January, little time was left for gathering the necessary craft together and adapting them as required. To ensure there were no failures this time Deputy Commissariat General William Kay was instructed that on the following day he was to proceed to Braunston, but on his way he was to call in at Blisworth[23] to see the agents of the various canal carrying companies at that point, the idea being to secure, if possible, up to ten narrow boats as the total of 2,028 men advised did not take into account the women and children nor the baggage; and furthermore, if boats could be supplied a day's march would be saved. Any other surplus craft should be requested to move down the canal to Braunston on the Oxford Canal. Every endeavour was to be made to ensure that boats were fitted out with seats and covered accommodation. Straw was also to be provided for the men to lay on at night whilst the boat was on the move. If, after all his efforts, he was still short of sufficient craft he was to show his letter of authority to a local magistrate, who would do what he could to make up the deficiency. Pickfords, it seemed, had only promised to supply ten out of the forty boats required. Kay was only to pay the usual rates which were to be certified by a magistrate, and he was to take £200 with him to pay the necessary expenses.

In the end it seems that the arrangements worked out better than had been expected. The 2nd Battalion was embarked at Blisworth, and to meet all the requirements for the 1st Battalion at Braunston it was only necessary to ask the Trent & Mersey Canal Company to prevail upon ten other boats to proceed to that point for loading. As expected the movement was strung out over a large part of the route, albeit a bit haphazardly, so it is not surprising therefore that this is reflected in the ultimate arrival times at Dublin. The 1st Battalion arrived on 9, 11 and 13 January 1804, while the 2nd arrived on 8, 10 and 16 January.

Once again it appears that Pickfords had not been entirely honest with Sir Brook Watson for the contract had been based on that which pertained for the Royal Staff Corps move, whereas in practice Pickfords had charged an extra 70 pence per boat. Perhaps the stipulation for exclusive use of each boat had something to do with the increased rate. In the final reckoning, Brook Watson agreed to pay the additional sum requested, provided the local magistrate, who was involved with the move, was in agreement and did sign the certificate.[24]

This next move arose when the Duke of York instructed his Quartermaster General (Major General Brownrigg) early in October 1804, that he was to make the necessary arrangements for the 2nd Battalion of 42nd Regiment of Foot (Royal Highland) to march from Braintree in Essex to Blisworth and there board narrow boats for Stockton Quay.[25] At the latter point, which is just five miles along the Bridgewater Canal after its junction with the Trent & Mersey Canal at Preston Brook, they were to march over London Road bridge, which spans the Mersey, and then through Warrington and so to Liverpool where they were to board vessels for Ireland. The unit consisted of 25 officers, 52 NCOs, 22 drummers and 805 other ranks, a total of 904 men. For this move the Deputy Commissariat General assigned to oversee the arrangements was Charles Dalrymple, and he was to be assisted by an officer of the Quartermaster General's department.[26] Once again Pickfords had contracted to supply the necessary craft, but one of the clauses allowed the military to use other carriers in the event of Pickfords being unable to meet the specification. The benches, which had been used on previous occasions, were to be moved by canal from Pickford's store at Braunston to Blisworth. In view of the numbers involved, and being sensible to the need to spread the move over three days and thus avoid congestion not only at the point of embarkation, but also at locks and tunnels along the line of route, it was therefore decided that loading should take place on Saturday 13 October, Monday 15 October and Tuesday 16 October. Sunday loading and movement was not normally permitted by the military unless emergency conditions existed, as determined by the Secretary of State in accordance with the relevant clauses in the Mutiny Act.

One item which the Commissariat had not bargained for, having regard to the time of year, was inadequate water supply for working boats on the Grand Junction Canal. However, Joseph Bullock, a Deputy Commissariat General, had seen the canal committee on the matter and got them to issue an order allowing the boats conveying soldiers to pass without 'waiting turns'.[27] This was a system often adopted at a flight of locks in dry weather in order to make the utmost use of water. Each boat requiring to proceed either up or down the locks, had to wait the arrival of a boat coming in the opposite direction, thus making sure that the maximum amount of traffic was passed for the water consumed.

Hardly had this move been completed and boats got back to their normal working, when orders came from Horse Guards on 26 November, for the 2nd Battalion of 92nd Regiment of Foot (Gordon Highlanders) consisting of 25 officers, 45 NCOs, 18 drummers and 680 other ranks, a total of 768 men, to proceed from Colchester on 29 and 30 November and 1 December to Blisworth on the same route to Ireland as that taken by the 42nd Regiment of Foot. As before, Dalrymple was to take charge of the operation at Blisworth, assisted by an officer from the Quartermaster General's department. The move apparently took place without a hitch as at long last the military and the canal authorities seem to have got their act properly together.

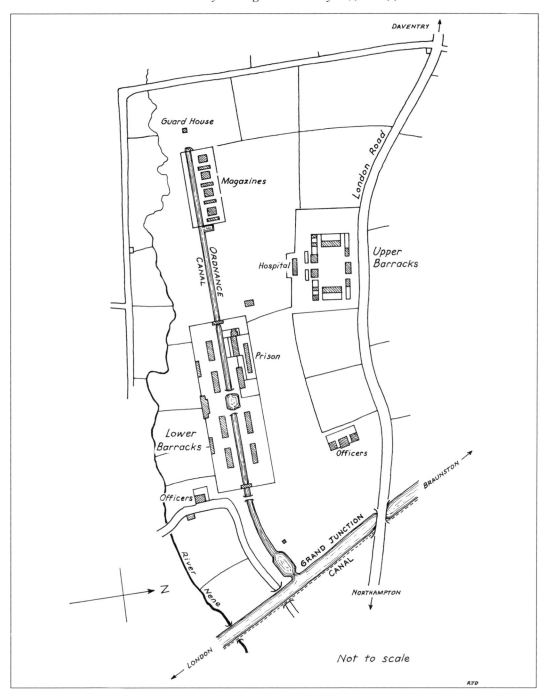

9. Weedon Barracks, Northamptonshire, 1835

CHAPTER TWO

Successes and Failures

WEEDON, in Northamptonshire, is said to be the centre of England and because of its proximity to the Grand Junction Canal and Watling Street was considered to be a suitable place at which to erect an Ordnance Depot, for the storage of all kinds of arms and ammunition well away from the coast where an invasion from France could be expected at any time. The enabling Acts of 1803 and 1804 for the construction of this depot on the 172 acre site, do not make any mention of a canal, but one of 5½ furlongs to connect with the Grand Junction Canal was built by a contractor with 33 staff, being completed in June 1806.

The arm of the canal into the depot commenced with an entrance basin (150' x 150') which was followed by a short length to a swing bridge. At this point the canal entered the depot proper through the brick perimeter wall under a guard house from which a portcullis gate was lowered into the canal when boats were not passing into or out of the depot. Beyond lay four two-storey warehouses on each side of the canal, capable of holding 250,000 muskets and 30 pieces of field artillery. Outside this compound was a barracks for 500 men of the artillery, plus a hospital (120' x 45'). After passing under another guard house, there followed an open space and then another portcullis which led into the magazine compound. Here to one side of the canal were four stores, each with a blast block in between for the storage of 5,000 barrels of gunpowder and small arms ammunition. As would be expected very little troop movement by canal took place to and from the Depot, except for those on escort duty. Regiments and detachments passing by the Depot did not stop here for refreshments or overnight stay. The Grand Junction Canal Company, in their Act of 1793, had generously allowed all military stores and personnel to pass free of tolls, but the construction of the Depot soon convinced them that more traffic was passing than they had originally envisaged with its consequent effect on water supplies. So much so that they obtained an Act in June 1805 requiring all military and naval stores to pass at standard rates; but if over 1,000 tons was moved in any one year a drawback was permitted. In July 1809 the Government were assembling an army in preparation to invade Flanders (Walcheren), and as part of this expedition the Board of Ordnance had arranged with Thomas Barnett of Weedon to move by canal 9,520 muskets which had been put into 476 chests by men of the Bedfordshire militia. These were loaded into four narrow boats to be taken to Paddington from which point they were to be conveyed by road to the Tower of London. The next the Board heard of this move was a message from the storekeeper at the Tower to say that part of the consignment was at the bottom of the Thames. Enquiries eventually elicited the fact that the carrier, William Green, had decided because of the need for great expedition, to divert to Brentford and tranship to barges there with a view to saving a day in transit. However, on floating down the Thames at one o'clock in the morning on the night of 27 July in a violent thunderstorm, the barge ran aground about three-quarters of a mile below Brentford, and sank.

The upshot of this incident was that a contract was awarded to Messrs Pickford to undertake this work in future for three shillings per hundredweight.

IRISH MOVES 1806–1807

The first recorded use of the route throughout from the Mersey to London, came about as a result of an instruction issued from Horse Guards on 19 July 1806 to the Duke of Gloucester, who was the officer commanding the North West District at Liverpool. In it he was ordered to gather together recruits coming from Ireland to join the 2nd Battalion of the 1st Regiment of Foot (Royal Scots) and when a suitable detachment was ready they were to proceed by canal to Paddington at which point they were to disembark and march to join their regiment at Horsham in West Sussex. [28]

In the event Captain V. Chisholm, together with Lieutenants J. Grant and A. McLachlane, shepherded 34 recruits from Liverpool on 15 August 1806, reaching Paddington seven days later. The canal carrier charged one guinea per person, plus £22 10s for their baggage. [29]

However, this can hardly be called making full use of the facility available and certain people in the media of the day thought likewise. Early in December a military correspondent on the *Morning Advertizer* suggested to the Secretary of State that canals should be used where practicable for the movement of troops, to save fatigue on long marches. Another idea he propounded was that artillery horses, when not required for military purposes, should be used to haul these boats. What he did not know was that all too soon the first part of his idea was going to be taken up with a vengeance. In Ireland the difficulties were coming to a head, so much so that law and order was rapidly breaking down even in Dublin. Atrocities were being reported

10. Weedon Ordnance depot, 1965. Constructed from 1806 onwards with its own canal link to the Grand Junction Canal. Close to Watling Street and only eight miles from Northampton, thought to be the centre of England, it was the terminus for many narrow boats loaded with gunpowder.

daily in the London newspapers and in desperation the Irish authorities appealed for assistance. The situation was deemed to be so grave that on 11 December 1806 the Cabinet agreed to send reinforcements straightaway by the quickest possible route. These were to consist of Major General Sir Arthur Wellesley's Brigade of Infantry, which was then located in Kent at Deal and Hythe. To ensure swift movement the Secretary at War issued instructions that this transfer was to take place under emergency conditions as defined in the Mutiny Act.[30] The newspapers were soon full of what was proposed; the first report appeared on 15 December in the *London Chronicle* wherein it was stated that the 3rd (East Kent/Buffs), 6th (Warwickshire), 7th (Royal Fusiliers) and 8th (King's) Regiments of Foot, consisting of 8,000 men, were expected to proceed in three separate divisions on Thursday, Friday and Saturday of that week, to London Paddington where they were to embark on canal boats for an eight day journey to Liverpool and then by sailing ship to Dublin. As sometimes happens newspaper reports are not always strictly accurate. The 6th Regiment of Foot (Warwickshire) was in fact ordered to travel by sea and the number of persons to travel by canal was only 2,614.

Orders now flew thick and fast from the Commissariat department. Firstly, Deputy Commissariat General R.H. Kennedy was told to proceed to Northampton with a view to looking after all the necessary arrangements for the workings north of Braunston as from 20 December and to travel with them to Runcorn.[31] His counterpart, L.B. Morse, was to look after the arrangements for the first part of the journey. Unlike normal marching on the public highway, troops when travelling by canal under emergency conditions had to be fed whilst the boats were on the move. Accordingly the bread contractor – Roger Partridge of 17 St Clements Inn, Strand, London – was advised on 17 December to provide at Paddington two days supplies for 500 men on 18 December, similarly for 1,000 men on the 19th and for a further 500 on the 20th. Not much notice! The supplier at Northampton got a little more warning, but he additionally had to transport these supplies 10¾

miles for which no doubt he had to hire a suitable number of waggons. Kennedy was given dispensation to increase the amount if found necessary. One cannot help feeling that the baker's ovens in the small county town of Northampton must suddenly have been put under considerable pressure.

Pickfords had agreed to supply 55 boats, at a charge of £30 each. Benches were to be supplied for the men to sit on during the day and straw for them to lie on at night.[32] The two Commissariat Generals were left in no doubt as to how to deal with any delays at locks, for they were instructed that in the unlikely event of this happening the full arm of the law should be invoked through a local magistrate. Woe betide any toll office clerk who did not wave them through! Kennedy must have 'posted' to Northampton for on the evening of the day on which he had received his instructions he was already reporting back by letter on the arrangements which he had put in hand with regard to bread and straw. The bread contractor at Stafford was given due warning of this urgent additional commitment when the boats were at Rugeley in Staffordshire, and similarly to J. North & Company of Chester, who were to deliver their supplies to Runcorn.

Whilst all this was going on it was decided to alter the brigade commander. Instead of Arthur Wellesley, who owned estates in Ireland, the post was given to Brigadier Robert McFarlane, who was told to proceed immediately to Paddington. Part of the 3rd Regiment of Foot (Buffs),who had recently arrived at Portsmouth from Guernsey and were recuperating from the boat journey in Hilsea barracks, were ordered to join their regiment at Paddington.

The embarkation, in the event, started one day late because some of the troops had been delayed on the road by exceptional wet weather, so much so that on arrival their clothing was wet through. So as a special consideration the Duke of York, who was watching the embarkation with the Duke of Sussex from the bridge by the toll office at Paddington, authorised the purchase of eight gallons of Gin at a cost of £4 5s 4d which was just enough to enable each man in the Royal Fusiliers to have a small mug.

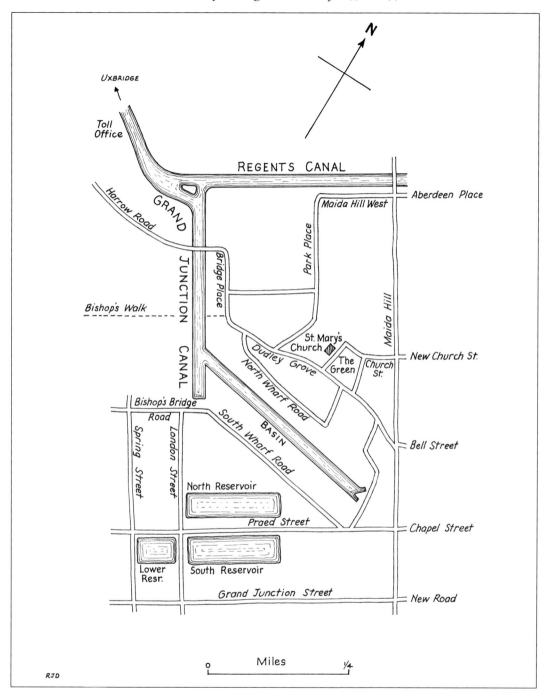

11. The Paddington Basin, London, 1828

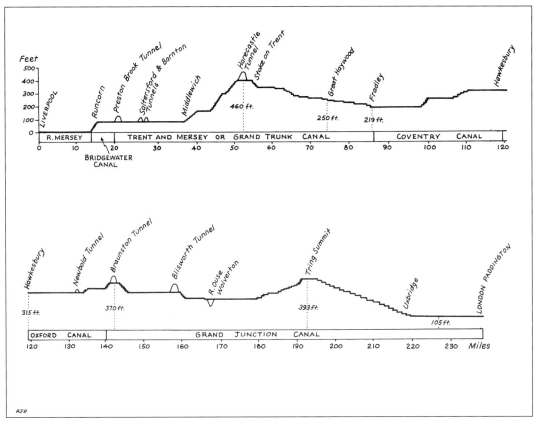

12. An elevation of the route from Liverpool to London, 1820

Generally speaking this very large move went off well, most of the boats reaching Runcorn in five days with the remainder arriving on the sixth day. From that point they moved down the Mersey on river craft.

Pickford's arrangements, considering the number of narrow boats involved, came out of it with credit, there being only one case where the Commissariat General accompanying the boats found it necessary to go to a local magistrate to impress some assistance. One can just imagine this highly paid officer rushing up and down the canal giving orders and seeing generally that everyone was doing their appointed task with the maximum amount of urgency. One horse drowned whilst hauling a boat-load of troops; perhaps the extra exertion was too much for the animal. When it was all over J.B. Morse got a

member of his staff to set down details of the expenditure and also what would have been incurred if the regiments had marched throughout by road *(see table 2)*. Surprise, surprise! The method adopted was £642 7s od cheaper! [33]

After much correspondence the benches on which the troops sat were eventually located in Pickford's yard at Manchester and arrangements were made for them to be returned to Paddington.

It will be recalled that in Chapter One mention was made of the fact that only the Grand Junction Canal had a clause in their Act which permitted troops and their associated baggage to pass free of toll. This anomaly was brought to the attention of the Board of Ordnance by Mr J. McDonald of 40 Lincoln's

TABLE 2: *Statement of the expenses incurred in conveying Brigadier McFarlane's Brigade by the Grand Junction Canal with what the marching money and hire of waggons would have amounted to had the troops marched from Paddington to Liverpool in December 1806 and January 1807*

	£	s	d
43 Boats for conveying 60 men each			
12 Boats for officers and Regimental Baggage – @ 4 each Battn			
55 Boats with Horses and Drivers @ £30	1,650	0	0
Carpenters Bill for 400 Benches	183	15	0

Straw delivered at:

	£	s	d
Paddington	25	4	0
Leighton	5	3	0
Braunston	12	2	6
Fazeley	1	16	0
Rudgley	2	14	0
	46	19	6

	£	s	d
8 Gallons Gin at Paddington, being a glass per man, given Fusiliers they having marched from Eltham, in heavy rain, and were wet through at the time of getting into the Boats.	4	5	4
Travelling expenses of Commissariat Officers with the several Divisions, who proceded the troops by land, in order to provide bread, straw and other necessities	79	6	11
NB. A claim has been made for the loss of a horse that was pressed and accidently drowned in the canal which if approved by the Lords Commissioners of His Majesties Treasuries will be added, it being customary to pay loss of this description	18	0	0
	1,982	6	9
Difference	642	7	0
	£2,624	13	9

The boats travelled night and day, part were five days and others six days on their route. The navigation by the canal ended at Runcorn upon the Mersey 18 miles from Liverpool, from Runcorn the troops were conveyed down the Mersey to the Transports on River craft which not being provided by the Commissariat Department, the expense cannot be stated.

	Sergeants Drummers Rank and File
Brigadier General McFarlane's Brigade:	

	Buffs	894
	Fusiliers	801
	Kings	840
	Men	2,535

	£	s	d
Extra allowance to Inn Keepers for 2,523 men for 15 marching and 2 halting days at 11d per day each man	1,975	3	9
Hire of 60 waggons being 20 per Battalion 215 miles at 1d per mile per waggon	645	0	0
Expense of warrants for impressing waggons supposing each regiment marches in two divisions	4	10	0
	£2,624	13	9

NB. Two waggons extra per Battalion were allowed in the above calculation, as the regiments had their new clothing to carry.

L.B.MORSE
Principal Deputy Commissariat General
In charge of Home District.

Inn Field, who suggested that the Mutiny Act should be altered to permit troops and baggage to pass free of tolls on all canals, irrespective of circumstances.[34] As far as can be ascertained there was no follow up.

Early in November 1807, as part of the general programme to change the units serving in Ireland, it was decided that the 2nd Battalion of 48th Regiment of Foot (Northamptonshire) should be moved from Epping in Essex to Liverpool where they were to embark on vessels for Dublin. In view of the success of the 1806 move from London by canal, the Government approached Pickford's office in Castle Inn, Wood Street, London, for their charge to convey 16 officers and 1,007 men from Blisworth to Runcorn.[35] The quotation must have been unacceptable as the unit marched throughout by road.

INTERNAL MOVEMENT PROBLEMS 1809

Sometimes those giving out marching orders in Horse Guards made classic blunders. A case in point concerns that issued on 27 July 1809, which required the 2nd Battalion of 6th Regiment of Foot (Warwickshire), who had only just arrived at Chatham from the Peninsula, to march to Paddington and there join canal boats for 'Preston'. A nice idea but the through route was not then available; perhaps the clerk when writing out the instruction had forgotten to insert the word 'Brook'; anyway on 1 August a hurried note was despatched to Paddington altering the boat destination to the nearest point, this being Stockton Quay on the Bridgwater Canal.[36] Whilst embarkation was taking place, a soldier deserted and three others got themselves discharged. It is not recorded how many boats were required for the 285 men plus their ten waggon loads of baggage, but the move appears to have gone off without a hitch.

The 37th Regiment of Foot (North Hampshire), after a long tour of duty in the West Indies, left Trinidad on 25 June aboard the troopship 'Felicite' which finally docked at Deptford in September. Soon after their disembarkation the four officers, six NCOs, two drummers and 106 other ranks, were instructed to march to Paddington where they were to board canal boats for Burton-on-Trent in Staffordshire.[37] As the Grand Union (Old) route from Norton Junction on the Grand Junction via Foxton to the Soar navigation was not yet open, they had to travel via the Oxford and Coventry Canals to Fradley junction at which point they turned east along the Trent & Mersey (Grand Trunk) Canal for nine miles through ten locks before reaching their destination. On 25 September the unit, under the command of Lt Col. William Spread, embarked on four boats provided by Pickfords and over the Grand Junction Canal they passed without any problems. However, on arrival at Braunston Stop-lock on the Oxford Canal a minor fracas took place as Pickford's staff were under the misapprehension that the move was being made under the auspices of the Mutiny Act and refused the toll-keeper's request for details. The senior officer took the matter into his own hands and the boats proceeded. The upshot was that Richard Tawney, the Oxford Canal's engineer and agent, who lived at Dunchurch near Rugby, penned a stiff letter to James Pickford, requesting 'payment be made in full and that in future his staff give proper details irrespective of circumstances'.[38]

CENSUS OF BOATS 1809

On 1 October 1809 Lt Col. James Willoughby Gordon was appointed Commissary-in-Chief of all forces except those in Ireland and the East Indies. Among the instructions issued to him by Lord Portland was one which required him to 'be fully informed of the different resources of the Country in Grain, Flour, Forage, Fuel, Mills, Ovens and Carriages and also the conditions of the roads and communications of Land Carriage and Inland Navigation'.[39] On 10 November, therefore, he sent out a general enquiry to all his District Commissariats in England, concerning inland navigation, and asked to be advised details of boats, crews, horses, etc. on each navigation, together with any other useful comments which might assist in determining their use for conveying troops *(see table 3)*. From examination of the returns it is obvious that the

TABLE 3: *Number of craft on English canals in 1809*

Aire & Calder 700	Ellesmere 200	Ouse (Yorkshire) 150
Ancholme 10	Foss 6	Oxford 193
Andover 10	Fossdyke 30	Rochdale 300
Ashton 200	Glamorganshire 50	Selby 100
Avon (Bath) 12	Grand Junction 130	Severn 300
Barnsley 10	Grantham 40	Shrewsbury 250
Basingstoke 30	Hereford & Gloucester 18	Somerset Coal 50
Birmingham 227	Horncastle 40	Staffs & Worcs 500
Birmingham & Fazeley 17	Huddersfield 10	Stainforth & Keadby 8
Brecon & Abergavenny 30	Itchen 10	Swansea 60
Bridgewater 111	Kennet & Avon 57	Thames & Severn 60
Bridgwater & Taunton 40	Lancaster 80	Trent 30
Calder & Hebble 200	Leeds & Liverpool 200	Trent & Mersey 400
Chester 50	Louth 18	Warwick & Birmingham 26
Coventry 115	Manchester, Bolton & Bury 40	Warwick & Napton 22
Croydon 22	Market Weighton 8	Wharfe 5
Dearne & Dove 10	Mersey & Irwell 47	Wilts & Berks 60
Derwent 30	Monmouthshire 60	Worcs & Birmingham 12
Don 50	Montgommery 100	Wye 102
Driffield 20	Neath 30	Wyrley & Essington 171
Droitwich 20	Ouse (Bedfordshire) 100	Yare 70
Dudley 50		

total number of craft quoted on each navigation may well be inaccurate in view of the distances over which a number of craft plied.[40]

CANAL FLY-BOATS 1810–1811

On canals a fly-boat system had been developed which was extensively used for the conveyance of small packages in competition with stage coaches and waggons on the roads. Usually these boats were drawn by two horses which were changed at frequent intervals. By this means an average of seven miles per hour, inclusive of lockage, was sometimes achieved. One, and sometimes both horses carried a postillion who assisted in working the locks and was adept at flattening himself down to his saddle as the horses dashed under low bridges.

These fly-boats also conveyed a limited number of passengers at very competitive rates, but travelling conditions left a lot to be desired.

Generally they had to sit among the goods with only a tarpaulin sheet to protect them from the elements. Even so, for the underprivileged such as soldiers, it was better than marching along a road which could be dusty or at worst made up of numerous pot-holes filled with water. There was also the fact that they had to put up at an inn, some of which were frequented by undesirables who would rob them, not to mention the highwayman.

On the fly-boats things were different as they started at fixed times, usually carried 15 tons or less of cargo and proceeded with all speed, night and day, to their destinations. With no time to stop for food and drink, all this had to be purchased in advance unless they were prepared to take their chance with quick service from a canal-side pub at a lock.

No doubt initially unauthorised use was made of canal fly-boats by small detachments and single men because the marching money allowance was based on the anticipated number of days which the journey would take marching along the roads. This, when set against the cost by canal boat because of its shortened journey time, was often cheaper. The army therefore saw that this arrangement should be regularised and so Lord Palmerston, who held the post of Secretary at War from 1810 to 1827 issued the undermentioned order:[41]

268 SECTION III. – PART 1

Regimental Accompts

Circular to Officers Commanding Corps at Home, relative to the Passage of Soldiers from one part of Great Britain to another, by Sea, or by Canals, when not on Pass or Furlough.

War-Office, 16th April, 1810.

SIR,

I HAVE the honour to acquaint you, that in those cases in which it may be judged advisable to send Non-Commissioned Officers and Men of the Regiment under your Command, from one part of Great Britain to another, by Sea, or by Canals, the Charge of their Passage will be allowed in the Public Accompts of the Regiment, provided the Expense should not exceed what would have been incurred had the Men marched by Land.

It is, however, to be clearly understood, that this Regulation only extends to those Men who are on Duty, and not to those on Pass or Furlough.

I have the honour to be,

Sir, &c.,

PALMERSTON.

In those days it was the army policy that, when units proceeded to destinations outside the United Kingdom, the number of women was restricted to one for every ten men. Therefore on embarkation a number of women with their children had to be returned to their place of birth, for which the Act passed on 26 June 1811 allowed the local magistrate to pay 2d per mile out of the poor funds, which was more than often spent on conveyance by canal fly-boat.[42]

ANTI-INVASION PREPARATIONS 1811

For some time the Army had been giving serious consideration as to the movement of reinforcements to the anticipated battle zone in the event of an invasion actually taking place. From their census of 1809, they had formed a picture of the location of canal boats on the various parts of the inland waterway system, but nevertheless they felt constrained, as borne out by the following paragraph from the book of instructions dated 1 January 1811:

In case of Invasion all the Boats upon the different canals must be at the disposal of the Commissariat for the purpose of passing magazines and supplies for the armies as far as that may be necessary, but no further, because the Common Business of the Country must meet with no interruption that can be avoided.

Therefore taking the foregoing into account, they restricted the movement of troops by canal to eight of the nine militia regiments based in the county of Staffordshire, who were to make their way to London to join what was to be known as the Thames Army.

4,000 men approximately were to march to Birmingham and there embark on canal boats. It seems reasonable to suppose that the troops would have boarded approximately 70 narrow boats and to avoid the congested part of the Birmingham Canal, known as Farmer's Bridge locks, that the actual point of loading would probably have been in the Sampson Road wharf area on the Warwick & Birmingham Canal. As the majority of craft would have been in the coal trade, some form of cleaning would have been required as well as the prompt manufacture of a number of benches to be placed longitudinally in the boat to enable the soldiers to be seated back to back.

Another 4,000 men approximately were to march to Litchfield, but as the Wyrley & Essington Canal was not heavily used by canal craft they would have in all probability marched three miles along the Burton-on-Trent road to where there was a wharf on the Coventry Canal on the main Manchester – London trunk route. In this particular case, as most of the craft would have been conveying merchandise traffic, no cleaning would have been required but the provision of benches would still have been necessary.

Contingency plans had been worked out in the event of the canal system being frozen. Those from Birmingham would have been moved in carriages and waggons, via Coventry, Rugby, Northampton, Newport Pagnell, Woburn, Luton and St Albans, and those from Litchfield via Hinckley, Lutterworth, Market Harborough, Higham Ferrers, Hitchin and Hatfield. It was estimated that both contingents would reach their destination in three days, but those by canal would have been in better shape for fighting as they would not have been worn out by a long march or by a distinctly bumpy coach ride. If every exertion had been made by the boatmen, canal workers, etc., the journey time could easily have been brought down to two days. Soldiers would, of course, have been expected to assist at locks with the fifes helping the men to pass their time away in the boats. Each soldier was required to carry in his pouch three days' supply of cooked food.

CAVALRY MOVES 1812–1813

Baggage and other impedimenta was generally moved in waggons or carts which had to be impressed through a magistrate or parish constable, a not very satisfactory arrangement. On occasions where it could be shown that there was some financial benefit to be gained, the heavy baggage was moved by canal, but then the question arose as to whether an escort should be provided as unfortunately a certain number of canal boatmen were known to be light-fingered. These conditions provided the first known instance when men from a cavalry regiment travelled by canal. This was in 1812 when, on 24 August 1812, an order was issued for the heavy baggage belonging to the 23rd Light Dragoons to be moved from Paddington to Stockton Quay.[43] Eight officers took advantage of this instruction by initially escorting the four waggons and three carts from Romford to Paddington and then travelling on the narrow boats. The next order concerns the 9th Regiment of Light Dragoons (Queen's Royal Lancers) who formed part of the rearguard when the army, under Lord Wellington, retired to Ciudad Rodrigo and was constantly engaged with the enemy. Many horses were lost from inclement weather and scarcity of forage. In the Spring it was ordered to transfer

most of its remaining horses to other regiments and return to England. It proceeded to Lisbon and embarked at Belem on 17 April 1813 on *Globe* and *Britannia,* and after a long sea voyage eventually reached Deptford on 17 May with only 39 horses.[44]

The Duke of York had already heard about their condition even before they had reached Deptford, so on 15 May he had requested that arrangements be made for the surviving 27 dismounted men to be moved by canal from Paddington to Blisworth. The chain of command acted quickly, since on the following day the Commissariat's General Office was able to advise the Quartermaster General that sufficient boats would be available on Tuesday, 18 May, at 2 pm. Such was the condition of the men, however, that their march with 20 tons of baggage from Deptford to Paddington took longer than had been expected, so that departure had to be deferred till 19 May at 12 noon which gave more time to the bread supplier, who was to issue them with two days' rations. No doubt the troops enjoyed their relaxation on this two-day journey which went off satisfactorily without any further problems.[45]

A FLURRY OF ACTIVITY 1814

At the commencement of 1814, the British Army was fighting in several parts of Europe with militia units being raised to supplement the regular army within the United Kingdom. Such was the rush of persons to join the militia that temporary arrangements were made for regiments of the line to raise a second battalion. The 22nd Regiment of Foot (Cheshire) had its second battalion placed on the establishment on 18 February. Next month the decision was taken to transfer this new battalion from Chester to Colchester, using canal transport for part of the journey. To start with, the Deputy Commissariat General at Liverpool was directed to negotiate with the boat owners in his area for the necessary transport to convey companies of troops, each made up of 100 men.[46] Alas, on 26 March Mr J.C. Herries, the Commissariat General in London, had to report to the Quartermaster General that the boat owners were unwilling to make the boats available because there was a back-log of goods in their warehouses waiting to go south as a result of the severe winter. Therefore there was nothing for it but for the battalion to march throughout by road.

A little while after they had arrived in Essex, orders were issued on 27 April for them to return to Chester.[47] Once again it was the intention to use canal transport for part of the route and on this occasion the Commissariat was successful. Mr Herries was, in fact, able to advise the Quartermaster General that, following his contact with Pickfords, two options were open to him. Either he could authorise the unit to embark at Paddington, for which the charge would be £300, or he could make them march all the way to Blisworth and embark at that point, in which case the charge would be reduced by £50.

In both instances the boat journey would terminate at Runcorn from which point the troops would have to march to Chester. Two days later, the Commissariat was advised that a slight compromise had been reached in as much as the point of embarkation would now be Stony Stratford situated on Watling Street in Northamptonshire, with the terminating point being Preston Brook which lies below the hilltop village of Preston-on-the-Hill. Not only did this reduce the canal journey in Cheshire by 5½ miles, but the road mileage too by one mile to 14 miles, which could be marched in one day. Eventually early on the morning of 29 April, six boats were made available and the loading took place under the watchful eye of the Commissariat officer for the county of Northamptonshire. So, in the end, the soldiers of the newly formed 2nd Battalion got a taste of being moved by canal; however the battalion did not see much further service as it was disbanded on 24 October 1815.

Up to now the main thrust seems to have been up the canal route from the South East to the North West, but suddenly this was to change when a marching order was issued on 30 July [48] which envisaged the 47th Regiment of Foot (Lancashire), consisting of five officers, 15 NCOs and 129 other ranks travelling by canal from Hull to Liverpool. The trans-Pennine canal route, the Rochdale Canal, had been opened in 1798, but it involved heavy lockage in a comparatively short distance, 18 in Yorkshire and a further 30 in Lancashire before reaching the town of Rochdale. So it would have taken longer for the soldiers to have travelled throughout by canal than the conventional marching by road. Therefore it is not surprising to find from examination of Regimental records, that a good oldfashioned compromise was reached. The vessels from Hull took them up the Yorkshire Ouse, onto the Aire & Calder Canal, before finishing at Salter Hebble bridge on the Calder & Hebble Canal which is situated some 1¾ miles from Halifax. From this point they marched over the Pennines to Rochdale where the unit was quartered, until eventually orders were received for the final part of the journey to Liverpool.

No sooner had this move been completed than a request was received from the Quarter Master General, dated 23 August, for the 2nd Battalion of 34th Regiment of Foot (Cumberland) consisting of 13 officers, 18 NCOs and 217 other ranks, to travel by canal between the same two points en route for Ireland. With the experience gained from the previous move Mr J.C. Herries was soon able to set the wheels in motion for a second contingent.[49] In fact he was able to advise the Quartermaster General on 1 September, that the boats had already been supplied. In the absence of any detailed regimental records it has to be assumed that the troops travelled by the same route as the 47th.

CHAPTER THREE

The Brigade of Guards

O N 4 December 1821, the familiar orders rang out over the parade ground of Knightsbridge Barracks in London, and the whole 3rd Battalion of 1st Regiment of Foot Guards followed the band and their mounted officers. Recently entitled to be known as The Grenadiers, they marched out across Hyde Park then down Edgware Road to Paddington Basin on the Grand Junction Canal, cheered on by 'an immense concourse of people'.

This move followed hard upon the visit of King George IV to Dublin earlier that year when he was less than satisfied with the bearing of the regiments of the line stationed there.

Shortly afterwards, on 17 November 1821, the Rt Hon. Charles Grant, Chief Secretary for Ireland, wrote formally from Dublin to ask the Home Secretary, Lord Sidmouth, for a battalion of the Guards. The latter was taken aback by this request in view of the reduced number of troops under arms in England, and he felt that the matter should be referred to the Cabinet. After seeking the further advice of the Lord Lieu-tenant, the scene was set for a Guards battalion to be quartered permanently in Dublin, and this practice was to continue until 1848.

That Cabinet decision was taken on Saturday, 1 December 1821, when we read in *The News* that throughout the day Lord Palmerston as Secretary at War had been 'busily employed at his office in the Horse Guards' and Lord Sidmouth had come up specially from Richmond to be at the Home Office. Even HRH Duke of York was at his desk in York House as Commander-in-Chief, and with him was Major-General Sir Herbert Taylor. It was later revealed that this weekend

'bustle observable' in these offices related to the distressful state of Ireland.

Consequent upon these deliberations Sir Herbert Taylor wrote that day to Lord Sidmouth as follows:

I am directed by the Commander-in-Chief to acquaint your Lordship that the 3rd Battn. Grenadier Guards, consisting of 600 Officers, N.C. Officers & Privates, 1559 Firelocks, will embark at Paddington in Canal Boats on Tuesday morning if possible & be conveyed to Liverpool in about 6 days, thence to proceed to Dublin. Application is made to the Treasury for Canal Boats and to the Navy Board for Tonnage at Liverpool. The Battalion is commanded by Colonel Woodford, in the absence of Colonel Jones who is abroad[50] and it will remain under the orders of Colonel Woodford.

The 2nd Battn. of the Grenadier Guards from Windsor will replace the 3rd Battn. in London, ...

This is the best arrangement which could be made with a view to Convenience and Expedition, and HRH trusts that it will be satisfactory to your Lordship...

There followed a dramatic postscript:

The Duke of Wellington has just been here to desire that I would mention to the Commander-in-Chief that, upon further consideration, it had occurred to your Lordship & to him that it would not be advisable to send this only remaining Battalion at once to Dublin but that it was desired that it should proceed to Liverpool or Bristol & there remain until further orders which may not demand its proceeding to Ireland if the Alarm of the Irish Government should in the meantime subside. The orders to the Navy Board for Tonnage at Liverpool are therefore recalled, and the remaining arrangements will take their course, Liverpool being in all respects the more convenient point of Embarkation and Tonnage being to be promised there at a day's notice.[51]

Accordingly, on that same day orders were sent to the '3rd Battalion of First or Grenadier Regiment of Foot Guards' in Knightsbridge Barracks. These orders were so unexpected that most of the officers were 'absent on visits or out of town; but expresses were instantly forwarded to them to be at their posts immediately'.[52] The newspapers, whilst not mentioning Dublin as their destination, did state that they were to proceed by the canal to Liverpool. The commanding officer's name was given as 'Hon. William Stuart' while later evidence shows it to have been Lt Colonel Sir John G. Woodford as in Taylor's letter. As for reporting on 'between 700 and 800 men', the total of 670 was on the Disembarkation Return dated 15 December completed by the Colonel on arrival in Dublin. In accordance with the regulations, this total included 20 women and 2 children.

We may take it that there were about 40 men in each narrow boat, that is about 20 craft in readiness, each with a Captain and bargemen and two horses.

About 200 men stopped for one day (9 December) at Nuneaton 'on their passage'[53] and the remainder would have halted at other points. This was because the next day being a Sunday they would have observed the terms of the standard Route or marching order which required troops on the march to halt on Sundays except in emergencies.

Once again on the move, with fresh bread supplied by the local Assistant Commissary General to replace the initial three days' supply, the Battalion would have completed their journey to the packetboats at Liverpool. On the 14th they embarked on the *Duchess of Atholl, Ocean, William, Hannah* and *Express,* reaching Dublin the next day. These vessels carried five horses for ceremonial duties.

The Grenadiers, who had traversed England by canal for Liverpool for the sea crossing to Dublin, returned seven months later by the same route, and every year for the next six years other Guardsmen were to follow their example.

On 19 July 1822 the stern instruction had gone out from the Horse Guards that 'it is intended immediately to withdraw the 3rd Battalion of Grenadier Guards from the Irish Establishment and to replace it by the 1st Battalion of that Corps'.

On the evening of Wednesday, 24 July 1822, Messrs Pickford, the carriers, had 26 boats out of their total fleet of 83, lying in the City Road Basin, London, of the Regent's Canal, ready to carry the Battalion's 20 officers, 710 other ranks and 23 women.[54] The events of that night were recorded by *The News*, which started badly by referring to '800 men belonging to the 3rd Regiment of Guard'. However, the paper gave an informative account of the action in City Road Basin, the largest of its kind on Regent's Canal, as told in the Hatton Garden Magistrates' Court:

George Porter, Edward Wray, Samuel Wilkins, Richard Blake, Robert Pritty and James Hadley, six athletic fellows, bargemen in the employ of Messrs Pickford & Co., the carriers, at the Regent's Canal, were brought up on Thursday, after a desperate conflict on a charge of conspiracy, combination[55] and riot...

A full account of this 'desperate conflict' appeared in *The Times* of 23 September 1822, recording the Conspiracy trial heard in the Middlesex Sessions on Saturday 21 September (with slight differences in spelling and four additional names):

George Porter, James Hadley, Robert Pritty, Richard Blake, Samuel Wilkinson, Edward Rea, Joseph Maxfield, Thomas Owens, William Pickering and Peter Hand were indicted for a conspiracy in the parish of St. Mary, Islington.

Mr. WALFORD stated the case for the prosecution. The prosecutors, he said, were Messrs Pickford who were extensive carriers on the canal; the prisoners were labourers in their employment, and the conspiracy charged against the prisoners was entered into for the purpose of compelling Messrs Pickford to raise their wages and preventing them employing other persons. Mr. Walford proceeded to state the facts as they were afterwards proved in evidence.

John Wright examined – Witness is clerk to Pickford & Co. who are extensive carriers and proprietors of boats on the canals. In July last Messrs Pickford entered into a contract with government to carry a battalion of the Guards to Ireland (in 26 fly-boats). On 25 July several barges belonging to the prosecutors with troops on board entered the basin of the Paddington Canal from the Regent's Canal about 12 o'clock at night. The prisoner, George Porter, came to witness and said no boat should pass the lock till their wages were raised to ten shillings a week: others joined in saying the same thing, and all cried out that they would knock out any man's brains who attempted to move any of the boats. The prisoners threw one man into the canal who was going with the boats. Two police officers came, and the prisoners were taken into custody. The number of men that joined in refusing to let the boats proceed was upwards of 100: the prisoners were selected for prosecution as being the most violent.

John Golden, agent for the Regent's Canal Company, stated that Rae gave the signal for the riot, crying out 'Now is the time, my lads!' Almost all the crews immediately came out of the boats, and refused to proceed unless their wages were raised to 10s per week. They then searched the boats, and took out a few of the men who were willing to do their duty, and threw one of them into the canal. The riot commenced about half past 11 o'clock at night, and continued until four in the morning.

Lomas, a toll-keeper on the canal, corroborated the evidence of the former witnesses.

William Thistleton, a police officer, stated he was called on and reached Paddington between five and six o'clock in the morning of the riot, when he took six of the prisoners into custody; he sent into Warwickshire after the other four and apprehended them there.

Mr. Wright was asked what wages the prisoners had at the time they struck for wages, and he replied they had from 7s to 10s a week and their board.

The case for the prisoners closed here.

The prisoners had no counsel, and called no witnesses.

The jury found a verdict of Guilty against all the prisoners.

The Counsel for the prosecution addressed the Court, and said he was instructed to pray for an exemplary punishment. The prosecutor's men had sometime before struck for wages, and were forgiven on a promise of future good behaviour; and the return they made was to take advantage of their employers having entered into a contract with the Government for the conveyance of troops, when they supposed their demands must be complied with.

The prisoners were sentenced to different periods of imprisonment from 1 to 3 months in a house of correction.

As a consequence of the riot, the embarkation of the Grenadiers was delayed for five hours, but they still managed to reach Liverpool on 31 July and to arrive in Dublin three days later. En route they had stopped at the canalside town of

Nuneaton on Sunday 27 July, in accordance with normal practice. The journey must have been uncomfortable as they had experienced heavy rain and hail, which was unusual for the time of year.

The 3rd Battalion of the same regiment left Dublin on 12 August 1822, stopped at Nuneaton and reached Paddington on 20 August. Travelling with this battalion were as many as 49 women and 31 children.

Twelve months later, a similar exchange was effected without incident, again thanks to the flyboats of Messrs Pickford & Co. On Friday 25 July 1823, the 1st Battalion Coldstream Guards (eight companies) under Lt Colonel Sir H.F. Bouverie KCB, marched out of the Tower of London, consisting of 20 officers and 591 other ranks. They were inspected by Colonel Woodford before they embarked at Paddington in 25 fly-boats.[56] Consequent upon this inspection the following congratulatory order was issued by Regimental Headquarters:

Colonel Woodford desires to express the satisfaction he felt at witnessing the highly creditable manner in which the 1st Battalion turned out for embarkation this morning; he has particularly to notice the sobriety of the men and the activity and propriety with which the Non-Commissioned Officers performed their duties, and he has made a favourable report to the Duke of York on the subject.[57]

Sunday 27 July was spent at Nuneaton by the 5th and 6th Light Infantry companies under Lt Colonel Hon. Sir John Walpole with the 3rd and 4th companies at Atherstone under Lt Colonel John Hamilton and the remainder at Tamworth. They all arrived at Liverpool on 31 July, eventually sailing for Dublin on Sunday 3 August.[58]

Once in Dublin, the Coldstream relieved the 1st Battalion Grenadier Guards commanded by Lt Colonel Delancy Barclay CB. They reached Liverpool on Thursday 7 August and then embarked in 28 of Messrs Pickford's fly-boats (some of their number spending twelve hours in Nuneaton on 10 August) to arrive in Paddington Basin on 13 August. Palmerston ordered them to occupy the King's Mews Barracks. As not all the men were in the barracks, officers were to ensure that those men going into billets 'take care to behave themselves regularly and duly pay their Landlords'.[59]

Next summer it became the turn of the Scots Guards to send a battalion to Dublin. They evidently were not going to be outdone by their Sassenach counterparts, for on 20 July 1824 instructions were issued to the effect that all officers of the 1st Battalion were required to march with their companies to the boats five days later, and in the meantime they were not to leave Town without the Commanding Officer's permission. Two days later the point of embarkation – 'The Canal Wharf, Paddington' – was mentioned in Orders coupled with the fact that the boats were for 'Conveyance to Liverpool'.[60]

The Commanding Officer on this occasion desired that his officers who had been given leave from the Battalion should clearly explain to their servants that they would receive pay as on the Irish Establishment.

On 24 July the Battalion paraded at King's Mews Barracks in Marching Order at 10.30 am for rigorous inspection. Next day, in full Marching Order the Battalion fell in at 6 am with the officers in white overalls and blue greatcoats. The battalion consisted of 17 officers and 694 other ranks. They arrived at Liverpool on 31 July and sailed for Dublin next day.

In Dublin the Scots took over from 1st Battalion, Coldstream, who had had a stay in Ireland for almost twelve months. The Regimental Pay-lists show that allowances were paid to the Battalion commander, Lt Colonel Hon. Sir John Walpole, and to his ten subordinate officers for one day spent at Liverpool with 636 men and one day at Tamworth, 7th and 10th August respectively. In 28 fly-boats they arrived back at Paddington on 13 August 1824,[61] and marched into Knightsbridge Barracks.

In 1825 it came the turn of the 2nd Battalion Grenadier Guards to perform the duties in Dublin, and the usual arrangements were made for their conveyance in canal boats from Paddington to Liverpool with a stop-over on the way.[62] These preparations were up to requirements; but the results caused a degree of friction such as to be deemed at Regimental Headquarters to be 'deviating from the system of the Guards', culminating in the resignation of the officer concerned.

The Battalion left London early on Monday 25 July and although the first four companies had pushed on they still did not reach Glascote, some nine miles and eleven locks beyond Atherstone, till 11 pm on the Wednesday. This was too late to enable Captain Godfrey Thornton, who had travelled by coach from leave to join them, to arrange billets in the small town of Tamworth one mile away. Therefore the men had to sleep on the boats for another night. Not so all of the officers, for Captain J.J.W. Angerstein and Lieutenants F.P. Delme' Radcliffe, S.T.F. Henry Ongley and George Duncombe managed to find accommodation in a local inn. Next morning at 7 o'clock the four companies were marched by their sergeants, under the superintendence of the Drill-Sergeant, and billeted in Tamworth. The other four companies, meanwhile, had stopped at Atherstone and Nuneaton and had been billeted in the area on the day of their arrival.

Captain Thornton, who was in charge of the four leading companies, asked at what time the boats would be ready to leave and was advised that it would be 7.30 pm that Thursday evening. Accordingly he ordered the men to be paraded at 6 pm. This left sufficient time for the men to cook their provisions for the next three days, wash themselves and take a little rest, the weather being very hot for the time of year. Down at the boats the straw had to be changed and new supplies of bread taken on. Captain Thornton, in his efforts to see that the men were being properly looked after, had instructed his junior officers to inspect the billets and ascertain if the men had any grievances. After a while they reported back that there were no complaints of any kind.

Everything therefore appeared to be ship-shape and proceeding according to laid down plans when suddenly, at 1.30 pm, the Battalion Commander, Lt Colonel Leslie Grove Jones, appeared from Atherstone on horseback. He seemed appalled at what he saw and became very angry. He immediately issued instructions that the men were to be marched back to the boats even though they had not finished cooking their provisions for the next three days. The men quickly drank their beer and under the command of their officers made their way back to the boats. Not surprisingly two of the men were drunk and there was considerable grumbling in the ranks. It was still only 3 pm when they reached their boats; some got aboard and some remained on the canal bank. The officers walked along the line of boats and placated the men. A roll-call was taken and only one was found to be absent and he had been given permission to visit relations in the area. In fact he returned in time to board his boat before it moved off. Despite the intervention of Lt Colonel Jones, the boats were not under weigh till the pre-arranged time of 7.30 pm

Next day, Thursday, the boatmen refused to proceed as Lt Colonel Jones had broken his sword over one of them during a dispute. The situation was only restored by the intervention of Quartermaster John Payne. On Saturday, Liverpool eventually came into view and at 4 pm they reached their point of disembarkation. Within a short time they were aboard their boats for Dublin. Lt Colonel Jones reported his Battalion's arrival in Liverpool with a short letter which contained none of the events at Tamworth, but simply stated that one man had been slightly injured whilst passing through a tunnel and that all the officers to whom he had granted leave had joined him at Liverpool, no doubt after travelling by coach, and that the man who had been absent when the boats left London had joined them at Tamworth. On his arrival in Dublin Lt Colonel Jones issued, on 2 August, a lengthy Battalion Order to the effect that officers should share the duties and fatigues of their men, and then went on to state that 'Col. Jones could never have dreamt that an Officer who had attained the rank of Captain who had been eight or nine years in the Army, that he should leave men entrusted to his charge entirely in the care of the drill Sergeants and that he should go and seek repose in an Inn, and no further occupy himself with the men under his command left in boats at a considerable distance from the quarter he had obtained for himself'. It seems more than likely that the officer referred to was Captain Angerstein.

13. Lieutenant Colonel Leslie Grove Jones (1779–1839), Grenadier Guards, who following an altercation with a canal boatman etc was forced by the Duke of York to resign his commission in 1825.

The matter did not rest there, for on 30 October Lt Colonel Robert Ellison wrote a long letter to Colonel Hon. H.G.P. Townshend, Regimental Lt Colonel, giving all the facts in which he stated that following consultation with General Sir George Murray, Commander-in-Chief in Ireland, he agreed that the order should be expunged from the Regimental Order Book and that Lt Colonel Jones ought to be removed from the Regiment.[63] Matters soon moved quickly for only two days later he was submitting his resignation from the service.

The Grenadier Guards Battalion relieved the 1st Battalion Scots who returned to London by the same route, without as far as it is known any incident, arriving at Paddington on 8 August from which point they occupied Knightsbridge Barracks and 'that part of Upper Westminster contiguous thereto'.[64]

In the following July this Grenadier Battalion was relieved by the 2nd Coldstream Battalion which, in August 1827, gave place to the 3rd Grenadier Battalion.

1827 was destined to be quite an important year, since in various ways it heralded changes in the movement of troops between London and Ireland.

One of the problems on the canal route to Liverpool was the difficulty experienced in getting through Harecastle tunnel on the Trent & Mersey Canal in Staffordshire. It usually took two hours to 'leg' through this tunnel, but as it was only of narrow construction it was necessary to restrict south to north movement to the morning, with north to south taking place in the afternoon and in consequence normal military movement could be held up for several hours unless boats were passing on urgent business as defined in the Mutiny Act. To overcome this problem the Engineer, Thomas Telford, had been called in by the canal company who eventually agreed with him, in 1825, that the solution would be the provision of a duplicate tunnel of 2,926 yards.

Whilst this work was in progress a company called The London & Dublin Steam Marine Company, part of the City of Dublin Steam Packet Company, had arranged with the partners, Joseph Fletcher and William Fernall of Limehouse, London, to build a 151 ft long steam boat of 513 tons powered by a 160 hp engine, called *Shannon*. This vessel was registered on 24 January 1826, master W. Randell, for operation between London and Dublin. A sister ship

named *Thames* was delivered later in the same year. By March of 1827 it was being stated of the *Shannon* that after her eighth voyage, not withstanding the winter gales, she was achieving a round trip time of 22 days, including calls at Cowes and Falmouth in both directions.

The Coldstream Guards sensed that here perhaps was a new form of transport for troops which should be worthy of their investigation. However before actually making use of this additional facility, it would first be necessary to cost the present and proposed movements in detail and then submit the facts to Horse Guards for their approval. Accordingly on 21 March 1827 the figures were penned, based on a known requirement in the near future to move one officer and twenty other ranks from London to Dublin *(see table 4)*.

Nine days later the Horse Guards authorised this move by the new method of transport for the detachment, which was just as well since there was a stoppage on the Trent & Mersey Canal between Sunday 8 and Easter Monday, 16 April, to enable the new Harecastle tunnel to be brought into use. Accordingly on Sunday 8 April they marched down to the river Thames below London Bridge, and there boarded their ship for what must have seemed a delightful experience even though the other ranks had to stay on deck. The officer would, of course, have had a first class cabin. After a normal voyage the vessel arrived at North Wall, Dublin, on Good Friday, 13 April. The resultant bill was £37 5s; although higher than the estimate was nevertheless cheaper than that by canal and also quicker and in good weather more comfortable. This result had considerable ramifications as evidenced by a letter from Lord Palmerston on 23 July 1827 to Sir Herbert Taylor, then Deputy Secretary at War in the Canning administration. This letter included the following:

In calculating what reduction can safely be made, we must not forget that our forces at home has been rendered much more speedily applicable to the service of the whole of the United Kingdom by the Facility of steam communication with Ireland, and that instead of being obliged to measure, as we formerly did, the amount of force to be kept in each Island, by the possible demands which emergencies in each island

TABLE 4: *Comparison of the cost in 1827 between transporting troops from London to Dublin by canal or by sea using steam vessels.*

	Canal/Packet Boat	Steam Navigation Throughout
Officer (1)	£4 10 0	£3 13 0
Other ranks (20)	£22 10 0	£26 0 0
Baggage	£11 14 6	£2 0 0
Total	£38 14 6	£31 13 0

may create, and thus keeping in each island a reserved surplus to meet such emergencies beyond the force required for other purposes, we may now consider the two islands as being for military purposes united, and may keep one such reserved surplus to meet emergencies in both islands.

In fact, a reinforcement could now be sent from the South of England to many parts of Ireland as easily as could be to Scotland; and for other parts of England where troops are stationed it could reach Ireland much quicker than it could get to Scotland.

Whilst Lord Palmerston was correct in his thoughts, as he well knew, he had already set in train arrangements for the usual transposition of Guards battalions between England and Ireland: but on this occasion the move started from the Dublin end.

The 2nd Battalion of Coldstream Guards, under Colonel Daniel McKinnon, arrived in Liverpool aboard the Dublin Steam Packet Company's vessel *Birmingham* commanded by Captain Head, on 26 July 1827.[65] Next day they left for Paddington on canal boats; at Harecastle they did not have to wait but still had to be 'legged' through the old tunnel. The usual Sunday stop was made at Atherstone and Nuneaton, before arriving in London on 30 July where they disembarked and then marched off to Portman Street barracks followed by 14 waggons with their baggage.

This last sentence belies the fact that there would have been considerable hustle and bustle at Paddington to bring this into effect, for with three berths only available since Messrs Pickford now dealt with most of their London business at the City Road Basin on the Regent's Canal, coupled with the knowledge that on average the next horse drawn boat with its crew of four could be expected to arrive approximately every ten minutes, therefore within a span of thirty minutes soldiers had to disembark, the boatmen had to take their two horses to the stables and then assist the shore staff with unloading the baggage and place it in the waggons, finally drawing the boat away from the wharf to another location to enable cleaning, etc. to be carried out. Time was of the essence, since the whole fleet which brought the Coldstream Guards southwards was required in 48 hours to

14. Henry John Temple, 3rd Viscount Palmerston (1784–1865), who, as Secretary at War from 1809 to 1831, was responsible for the general ordering of troop movement by canal.

do a similar journey northwards with the 3rd Battalion of Grenadier Guards.

Those officers who accompanied the men on the canal journey, were normally given a special boat to themselves. At this time it is possible that the boat, which had been formerly used by one of Pickford's partners – Joseph Baxendale – for inspection purposes, called *Joseph*, would have been made available to the officers.

Eleven officers from the Grenadier Guards' barracks at Knightsbridge made use of this facility when the 3rd Battalion set off from Paddington on 1 August 1827, under command of Colonel Woodford, and the remaining seven officers travelled direct by coach to Liverpool. The officers on the canal trip were expected to ensure that the men behaved themselves and also to see that they were properly looked after when the boats made their usual Sunday stop at Atherstone and Nuneaton. The journey progressed satisfactorily, especially as they were allowed to be towed through the new tunnel at Harecastle as it had a towing path unlike the old one. The 8 August saw them aboard the *Hibernia* and *Commerce* at Liverpool, and so ended the last whole battalion move by canal within the Brigade of Guards.[66]

AID TO THE CIVIL POWER: MANCHESTER 1826

During April 1826, the cotton and silk weaving industries in the Lancashire area were in a mounting state of unrest, so much so that a Cabinet meeting was convened on Saturday 30 April, to discuss the matter. Apparently the army authorities had got an indication as to the likely outcome for on Friday, 29 April, the Order Book of the Scots Guards records:

1st Battalion will march from Windsor to Knightsbridge on Monday next and hold itself in readiness for embarkation for Liverpool.

The Cabinet meeting took place at the London residence of the Prime Minister, Lord Liverpool; and Wheeler's *Manchester Chronicle* on the following Saturday sets out what transpired:

There were present Mr. Secretary Peel, the Chancellor of the Exchequer, the Earl of Harrowby, the Duke of Wellington, Viscount Melville, etc. They continued in deliberation till 12.30 when Mr. Secretary Peel returned to his Office, where he was closely engaged the rest of the day. Messengers were despatched from the Home Office in various directions. The Duke of York arrived in town at 3.00 p.m. from Newmarket and proceeded with all haste to his Office in Horse Guards, where Mr. Secretary Peel waited upon the Royal Duke, to lay before him, the information he had received from Lancashire, on the riotous proceedings of the Cotton Weavers in various parts, and also the results of the deliberations of the Cabinet Ministers, which had engaged their attention till after 5.00 p.m., assisted by Sir Herbert Taylor, Military Secretary to the Commander-in-Chief. Among the military arrangements agreed upon was, that the 2nd Battalion of the Coldstream Regiment of Foot Guards and the 36th Regiment should leave London for Manchester immediately.

The Duke of York proceeded to the King's Palace in Pall Mall to report to His Majesty the particulars of the proceedings. In the evening, Mr. Bailey, the King's Messenger, was sent off with despatches to General Sir John Byng to take command of the Manchester District.

For his part Mr Secretary Peel had given thought to the companies' annual programme of canal maintenance usually set for the first two weeks of May. With this thought in mind, he wrote immediately to the canal companies concerned, in the hope that they would all agree to postpone these works until after the Scots Guards had passed through their systems.[67]

This request was acceded to, and the 1st Battalion Scots Guards, who were already under orders to march into London, were advised on 2 May 1826 that on the following day they were to embark at Paddington for Manchester at 12 noon. The officers on the boats were Lt Colonel Charles Hall, two captains, six lieutenants and an adjutant. The remainder of the officers were to join at Atherstone.

They passed through Nuneaton on 5 May and would have disembarked in Manchester at Messrs Pickford's wharf in Bridgwater Street on the link between Bridgwater and Rochdale Canals. The strength of the battalion was approximately 700 men. They were initially billeted in Warrington before moving on to Manchester in November and over Christmas they marched back to London.

Initially, the 2nd Battalion of Coldstream Guards made all the necessary preparations for their journey to Lancashire, including the cooking of provisions to last them for three days, as it being an emergency move they would be travelling by day and by night.[68]

Eventually, on 13 May 1826, the eight companies left Paddington Basin in a hastily assembled flotilla of narrow boats, consisting of 21 officers and 635 other ranks.[69] They travelled 260 miles. The distance by road was 182½ miles;[70] but although this would have been a shorter distance, the journey time would have been longer in view of the need for the soldiers to rest overnight.

Apparently not all men were on parade when the unit left Paddington, doubtless they were sick or on leave, since the Coldstream Letter Books show that the undermentioned detach-

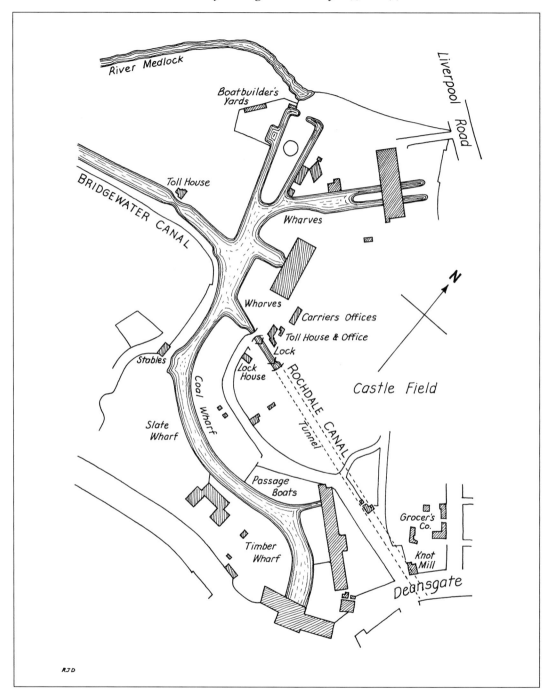

Labels on map: River Medlock, Boatbuilder's Yards, Liverpool Road, Toll House, BRIDGEWATER CANAL, Wharves, Wharves, Carriers Offices, Toll House & Office, Lock, Stables, Lock House, ROCHDALE CANAL, Castle Field, Coal Wharf, Slate Wharf, Tunnel, Passage Boats, Grocer's Co., Timber Wharf, Knot Mill, Deansgate, N

RJD

15. The Castlefield junction where the Bridgewater and Rochdale Canals met in Manchester, 1825

ments came on afterwards in scheduled fly-boat services. On Monday 26 June, one sergeant, one corporal and eighteen privates with about two tons of baggage, left London for Manchester; to be followed on 14 July by another party consisting of Captain the Hon. Thomas Ashburnham, one sergeant, one corporal and 41 privates. The non-commissioned officers returned to London by similar conveyance, no doubt to prepare for the unit's impending move to Dublin. It is interesting to note that the Quarter-Master General authorised the issue of blankets and haversacks for this detachment.

The battalion did not stay long in Manchester, for on 24 July it marched to Liverpool and embarked for Dublin to relieve 2nd Battalion Grenadier Guards.

SMALL PARTIES 1826–1839

For many years the privilege of travelling by coach had been available only to officers when not accompanying their troops. However this changed on 19 January 1827, when orders were issued from Horse Guards[71] to the effect that other ranks, including recruits and those under escort, could travel by stage-coach and indeed under certain circumstances private coaches could be impressed. However the relaxation in the general instructions was restricted to the Foot Guards and then only when it was not possible to travel by canal fly-boat. Examination of the Coldstream Guards' records show that during the six months ending 24 June 1830, 20 soldiers travelled by coach. In point of fact there are cases of travel between points over which canal fly-boats operated, but at the time the journey was made, the relevant canal was either frozen up or closed for annual maintenance.

The Guards regiments continued to give some support to canal transport *(see table 5)*.

Whilst all these small parties seem to have proceeded satisfactorily, there was one other which in its way demonstrates some of the problems associated with troops on the march. This case concerns Private John Ashton of the Coldstream Guards, who had travelled north by canal to Preston Brook in September 1837 to

TABLE 5: *Number of Guardsmen, their Women and Children who travelled by Canal*

YEAR	GRENADIER GUARDS[72]	COLDSTREAM GUARDS[73]	SCOTS GUARDS[74]	TOTAL
1828	1	98	1	100
1829	12	52	–	64
1830	15	–	9	24
1831	1	–	1	2
1832	1	–	–	1
1833	–	13	2	15
1834	8	13	2	15
1835	23	6	1	30
1836	2	4	3	9
1837	1	24	2	27
1838	7	8	5	20
1839	1	–	1	2
TOTAL	72	218	32	322

16. Preston Brook *c.* 1910, Trent & Mersey Canal. The nearest point to the military garrison city of Chester.

assist with recruiting in the Chester area. In December he received orders to return to the Depot in London by canal with his recruits. They duly set off on foot to Preston Brook where they expected to be billeted in a private house for the night before joining Pickford's fly-boat. However, the Parish Constable refused to find them accommodation so they had to put up at an inn instead. Billeting had of course been a bone of contention with the public for centuries, even though the Acts made in the Stuart period specifically stated that troops could be billeted only with the specific consent of the inhabitants. Each year the Mutiny Act was repassed by Parliament and the soldiers could be billeted in private houses only within one mile of the place stated on the marching route instructions.

Failing that they had to be placed in an inn. For the army authorities, who were very keen on counting the pennies, the latter course of action was to be deprecated. The reason is only too clear when it is realised that at a private house the charge was only a halfpenny per day for which the inhabitant was required to supply only candles, vinegar and salt, plus use of a fire and utensils for cooking and eating their food. Whereas at an inn, the situation was very different. Here for 10d the landlord was required to supply 1¼lb of meat, 1lb of bread, 1lb of potatoes and vegetables, all as a hot meal plus two pints of small beer and salt, pepper and vinegar.

Not surprisingly, when Private Ashton presented his bills for payment in the Regimental

17. Casier Lock at Birdham on the Portsmouth & Arundel Canal in 1905, through which a large detachment of the Coldstream Guards passed in 1838.

Depot there was some consternation at the amount involved. The matter was referred to the local magistrate who, when asking the Parish Constable for his comments on the matter, stated that 'Not once during his 30/40 years as the Constable for Preston Brook had he been requested to provide Billets for soldiers on the march'. No doubt he was given suitable advice as to the future, and one can only assume that because of the relatively low number of troops embarking and disembarking at that point that normally there was no problem.[75]

CANADIAN EXPEDITION 1838

During Napoleon's wars and the years that followed, a continuous navigation was put together connecting the Thames at Weybridge with Portsmouth: it was completed in 1831.[76] It was this route that was adopted by the Coldstream Guards in consequence of the situation in Canada.

Disturbances in this colony had arisen from bitterness between French and British settlers, and this reached such intensity that in the autumn of 1837 it was decided to call in the army to maintain the Queen's peace. The Guards had performed such duties in Manchester, but now it seemed more serious operations awaited them.

On 20 January 1838 an order from Horse Guards designated Major-General Sir James MacDonell KCH, to command the brigade made up of 2nd Battalion Grenadier Guards and 2nd Battalion Coldstream Guards, each battalion 800 rank and file strong. Arrangements for their departure were taken at a leisurely pace because it was known in London that the St Lawrence River was frozen over in winter. Lieutenant Hon. Louis Hope was transferred on 13 February from 1st to 2nd Battalion to take charge of the

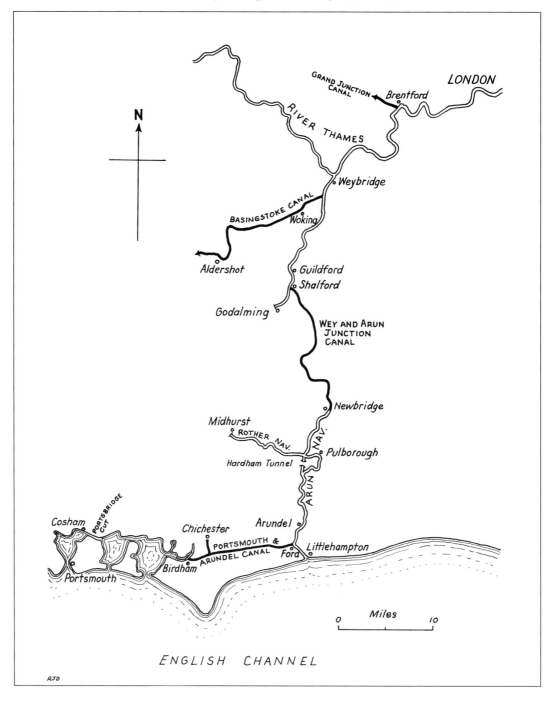

18. The London to Portsmouth route, 1837

regimental baggage. With him were Sergeants John Cullingford and John Sent, the former having had experience of travelling by canal some ten years previously; with them were 30 other ranks. They were to escort the baggage that was to be conveyed in canal barges from London to Gosport.[77]

Officers were to send 'all their heavy baggage to the Regimental Stores, Wellington Barracks, at or before 2 pm upon Thursday 22 March, after which time none will be received. They will also send a memo of the number of boxes or packages which they will send, with a description of each box or package, and specify which will be required on the voyage. Each package must be distinctly marked with their name in letters of inch long at least, and well and securely roped or secured. The Quarter-Master Sergeant has received orders to take in none others.'[78]

We next hear of the baggage party passing on the River Wey Navigation through Guildford on 30 March in two barges owned by the Portsmouth Lighter Company: *Rapid*, load 20 tons drawing 2'2" of water, and *Quicksilver*, load 18½ tons drew 2'0" of water.[79] Their tortuous route took them south to transit the South Downs in sight of Arundel Castle, then to Gosport.

As Lieutenant Hope's barges made their progress, the rest of the Battalion marched out of London on 28 and 29 March via Hounslow, Bagshot and Winchester to Gosport. There, on 17 April, they embarked on the transport *Apollo* and ship of war *Inconsistant* eventually making landfall at Quebec on 11 May 1838.

The 2nd Battalion of Grenadier Guards, however, marched throughout by road to Gosport with their heavy baggage, leaving London on 26 and 27 March.[80]

In retrospect, it appears that the Coldstream Guards made more use of English canals than the other two Guards regiments put together.

CHAPTER FOUR

Zenith

As far as can be ascertained there was one very important part of the British Army which, up to 1816, does not appear to have travelled by canal in England. This was the Royal Artillery, which did not come under the control of 'Horse Guards', but was in fact a totally separate organisation controlled by the Master General of the Ordnance. At this period the Master General was Henry 1st Earl of Mulgrave, an Irish Peer from New Ross in County Wexford, who held the post from 1810 to 1818. In 1816, as part of the scheme to reduce quickly the total establishment of the army, it had been decided that all persons of pensionable age should leave the service and as a large part of these had been stationed in Ireland it was necessary to replace them with persons from the depot at Woolwich. To this end arrangements had been made to issue the four companies with new uniforms, and when this had been done Lt General John MacLeod, Deputy Asst General, suggested on 27 May that they should be conveyed by canal from Paddington to Liverpool.[81] The Commandant, Lt General John Ramsey, had already been in touch with Messrs Pickford who had agreed to supply boats capable of carrying about 40 soldiers, plus their women, children, and baggage, at £50 per boat. The Board of Ordnance agreed the proposal and stipulated that the move should be carried out over two days with two companies embarking in five boats on each day. On 7 June the companies for the 7th and 10th Battalions left Paddington and arrived in Dublin twelve days later, followed on the next day by those for the 1st and 5th Battalions. 273 men plus 14 officers were involved,

who should have been under the charge of Major Foster but apparently this commitment for the canal journey was passed down to 2nd Captain William Twyning, who on arrival at Liverpool was to hand over to 2nd Captain Falkner Hope, whilst he himself returned to Woolwich by coach. On arrival at Dublin the four companies marched off to their respective destinations at Athlone, Ballincollig (near Tralee), Limerick and Island Bridge, just outside Dublin. Officers in the Royal Artillery were in the main more professional, since they were not allowed to purchase their rank but had to earn it either by merit or seniority.

Following upon the success of this move the Royal Artillery, in 1817, decided to use canal transport for a slightly different reason. Earlier in the year a gunner from 8th Battalion, who had absconded with some of the regimental funds, was brought back to England from France. As the unit concerned was now in Ireland, together with the associated papers on the case, the Board agreed the desirability of sending him over there. Presumably there was a very real chance that he might escape if he marched throughout by road, indeed some of the local populace might take pity on him and try to assist in his endeavour; therefore the decision was taken to send him by canal, escorted by gunners who were in the process of being posted to Ireland. Initially it was ordered that the escort should consist of six gunners on their way to join the 5th Battalion under the command of Bombardier F. MacGillivray from the 2nd Battalion. In the end a further twelve gunners joined the detachment en route to the 2nd Battalion.[82] Pickfords did not provide a separate boat, the whole detachment in fact travelling on a scheduled fly-boat service at a charge of £8 8s 0d. There were obviously sufficient artillerymen available to watch and follow the prisoner at all times. The bombadier who belonged to the depot at Woolwich, was permitted to return there from Dublin by the same route.

One of the problems faced by all armies who have won their campaign and eventually, for political reasons, ceased to occupy the enemy territory, is the call to reduce public expenditure on the armed forces. The Artillery were no exception to this feature for in 1818 much correspondence passed between the Lords Bathurst, Liverpool and Sidmouth on this facet, which culminated in the decision to generally reduce each regiment by one company.

Into this scenario came the Duke of Wellington when he took up his appointment as Master General of the Board of Ordnance on 1 January 1819, which post he was to hold till 1827.

At one of his first meetings of the Board in Pall Mall, London, on 18 January, Lt General John MacLeod, Deputy Assistant General, referred to the reduced establishment in Ireland which would necessitate four companies coming to England (Woolwich) for disbandment and one going there as replacement, and he suggested that in view of the numbers involved it would be advantageous for those travelling via Liverpool to travel by canal. This was agreed and the necessary arrangements were put in hand.[83]

Later on at a Board meeting on 19 February, when it was agreed that a troop of the Royal Horse Artillery should be sent to Ireland from Woolwich, the travelling arrangements stipulated that those with horses should ride to Liverpool, but the unmounted soldiers together with all the Troop's baggage and women, should travel by canal. In detail the resultant moves by canal were as follows:

(a) On 6 February two companies, consisting of 9 officers and 133 other ranks under Major Lacey, left London in six narrow boats and after transferring into Packet boats at Liverpool reached Dublin on 16 February.

(b) Between 3 and 9 February three companies,

consisting of 6 officers and 195 other ranks under Major Thomas Paterson, left Dublin for Liverpool on 9 and 11 February in 7½ narrow boats to London. This sea voyage delay resulted in some canal boats being held up for as much as four days awaiting loading.[84]

(c) On 27 February a detachment, consisting of 27 unmounted men of the Royal Horse Artillery together with all the Troop's wives and baggage under a staff sergeant, left Paddington in three narrow boats, and after changing craft at Liverpool eventually reached Dublin on 8 March.

These narrow boats, of course, also carried the accompanying wives and children who, in some cases, exceeded the number of soldiers and also space had to be found for the accompanying baggage which could weigh as much as 4½ tons per boat. Hence the comparatively low number of soldiers to each boat.

But 'the chickens soon came home to roost' for, at a Board meeting on 17 March, Major Campbell, Garrison Quarter Master at Woolwich, had the unenviable task of presenting Messrs Pickford's bill. This was as under:

(a) Six boats at £50 each = £300
(b) 7½ boats at £50 each = £375
    Demurrage incurred at Liverpool = £25
(c) Three boats at £50 each = £150
    Total £850

What was actually said at the meeting one can only conjecture, but suffice to say that this appears to be the only time boats were hired on a sole use basis during the Iron Duke's term of office, but small numbers of men continued to pass on scheduled fly-boat services. The bill, of course, was agreed for payment through the usual channels which involved Messrs Greenwood & Cox passing the sum to the order of Major Campbell. Other costs were the approximate 15/- per boat for moving the baggage between Packet and narrow boat at Liverpool, plus the costs incurred in moving it again by road from Paddington to Woolwich. All in all the total cost was in the order of £900, large by even those days' standards, but quite astronomical if inflated to present day levels.

REGIMENTAL MOVES TO AND FROM PADDINGTON BASIN 1816–1822

On 26 May 1816, the first of several large scale movement instructions was issued. The first concerned the 3rd Battalion of 1st Regiment of Foot (Royal Scots) who had just arrived at Chatham from Canterbury. Their orders were to march to London in two divisions and quarter 279 men in Kensington Barracks, billet 300 men in Lambeth and Vauxhall with the remaining 100 men similarly in Newington and Walworth. On Sunday, 1 June, they were to march to Paddington and there join boats for their journey to Stockton Quay.[85] At the latter point they transferred to boats on the Mersey and so to Liverpool before embarking on vessels for Dublin.

Liverpool was a scene of great activity for on 5 June orders came for one officer and 21 other ranks of the 2nd Battalion of 56th Regiment of Foot (West Essex), who were in charge of the regimental baggage, to proceed direct from there by inland navigations to Paddington. A stop was to be made en route at Atherstone for the purpose of receiving fresh provisions and cooking the same. The remaining 216 men of the Battalion had first to march to Warrington in Lancashire, cross the Mersey, and at Stockton Quay on the Bridgewater Canal take to their boats for London. Again a stop was to be made for receiving provisions, etc. The forward half were to stop at Nuneaton with the rear half at Atherstone. The journey by canal, allowing for the stop, was remarkably quick as they left on 12 June and reached their destination on 17 June. From that point they marched to Chatham via Welling, Bexley, Crayford, Dartford and Greenhithe.

After a long sea voyage from India the 86th Regiment of Foot (Royal County Down) disembarked at Portsmouth and marched to Chichester. There they busied themselves with recruiting to fill the vacancies caused by transfers whilst the unit was overseas. Suddenly, without warning, they were ordered to march with all speed to Northamptonshire on Sunday, 9 April 1819. The 395 men left later that day and with commendable effort reached London in two days, where they were quartered in Lambeth and Paddington. On 12 April they embarked at the latter point on canal boats to Weedon Depot. No reason has been found for this sudden dash, but in view of the absence of further observations, can only conclude that all went according to plan.[86]

Shortly after the opening of the Regent's Canal in 1820, an order came from Horse Guards to the officer commanding a detachment of 90 men belonging to the 9th Lancers (who had left Nottingham by canal on 11 August with the regimental baggage) to move to London. Their journey would have taken them up the river Trent to its junction with the Loughborough Navigation, then onto the Leicester Navigation, before traversing the narrow Leicestershire and Northamptonshire Canal, which joined the Grand Junction at Norton Junction.

They were instructed that, on arrival on 15 August at Paddington, they were to disembark and be quartered there before marching on the next day to the barracks at Romford in Essex. However, someone somewhere decided differently, for examination of the regimental records show that the boats continued on through the Regent's Canal right down into Regent's Canal Dock and out onto the river Thames. Their journey on the tidal water was very short indeed for they entered the Limehouse Cut and then onto the river Lee, finishing at Bow/Stratford on 18 August.[87] The trip through the Regent's, etc. would seem to have taken rather longer than one would have expected, but perhaps there were still teething troubles on the canal of which we are not aware. This new unloading point brought the men within nine miles of their destination which could easily be marched in one day.

1822 saw major moves in both directions between Liverpool and London with the same craft being used for both journeys. Unlike previous movements the work was not undertaken by Messrs Pickford, but instead the contract was awarded to Messrs Holt and John Kenworthy of Manchester. As this firm had only 16 'fly-boat' licences on the Oxford Canal, a certain proportion of the work must have been subcontracted to other carriers. Indeed when tendering payment to the Oxford Canal Company in June they hinted that perhaps some of the boats were passing under the auspices of the Mutiny Act and therefore no charge should be levied, but the canal company stated that this was not the case as no such prior notification had been received.

The initial move started in Ireland way back in January, when the 44th Regiment of Foot (East Essex) left Athlone for Dublin and on arrival were quartered in the Royal barracks. Eventually, on 6 April, 22 officers, 59 NCOs , 21 drummers and 583 other ranks, together with 115 women and 156 children (total 956) sailed for Liverpool. There on 11 April they transferred to 24 canal boats for Paddington, reaching London on 17 April. From there they marched to Chatham for a temporary rest whilst their transport to India was being prepared and the rearguard of the unit arrived from Ireland. The three outstanding officers left Liverpool by canal on 18 April, and finally on 7 May the eight other ranks followed suit. On 7 and 8 June they made their way to Gravesend where they boarded two East Indiamen ships *Warren Hastings* and *Winchelsea* for an eventful journey to Calcutta.

In the reverse direction the 71st Regiment of Foot (Highland Light Infantry) disembarked at Chatham on 17 April and five days later set off for a march to Paddington with their heavy baggage in 31 waggons, stopping en route at Dartford. On 25 April they left Paddington, stopping only to observe the Sunday at Tamworth, Atherstone and Nuneaton, arriving Liverpool on 1 May. Shortly afterwards they boarded a ship for Dublin.

So ended the only known example of a large troop movement being undertaken by Messrs Kenworthy.

THE ISLE OF MAN STORY 1822

The sovereignty of the Isle of Man was held by the Dukes of Atholl until 1765, when under the Revesting Act for the sum of £70,000 the situation was changed, but still left John Murray, the 4th Duke of Atholl, with extensive rights as the principal landowner on the island. In addition he was also Governor General from 1793 until his death in 1830.[88]

A small garrison of regular troops was normally maintained on the island to supplement the local force, with replacements being provided from time to time. Our story takes up when the last remaining regular troops, 40 men of the 29th Regiment of Foot (Worcestershire) left the island for Ireland in December 1821. The Duke, when he fully appreciated the state of the armed forces in the island, remembered that following the promulgation of the law in 1821 restraining the importation of foreign corn, the population of Peel had risen and drove out of the town a troop of yeomanry whom the Deemster had sent from Castletown to quell the riot. In addition, at Douglas disturbances had occurred, and great hardships were inflicted on the dealers in corn.

It is, therefore, not surprising that he asked his friend, Robert Peel, who was the Home Secretary, if a replacement detachment could be provided at an early date. After deliberation with the military authorities it was decided that there were insufficient men with the colours to meet even this small request, so the decision was taken to seek the King's sanction to a new force specially for service in the island. This unit was to be a veterans company, consisting of a captain, a lieutenant, an ensign, four sergeants, four corporals, two drummers and 76 privates; total 89. The whole package was put to George IV on 22 March and he graciously consented to the raising of this additional force, to be known as the 2nd Veterans Company.[89]

Speed was considered essential and it does credit to the army authorities of the day that it came into being as early as 25 April. The commander, instead of being a captain, was Major Albert D'Alton drawn from the 90th Regiment of Foot (Perthshire Volunteers). With him were Lieutenant Samuel Burgess from the 10th Royal Veterans Battalion, and Ensign John Walker from the 5th Royal Veterans Battalion. As other necessary preparations proceeded, the movement arrangements came up for consideration and the decision was taken for them to travel by canal.

Eventually, on 22 May 1822 they marched out

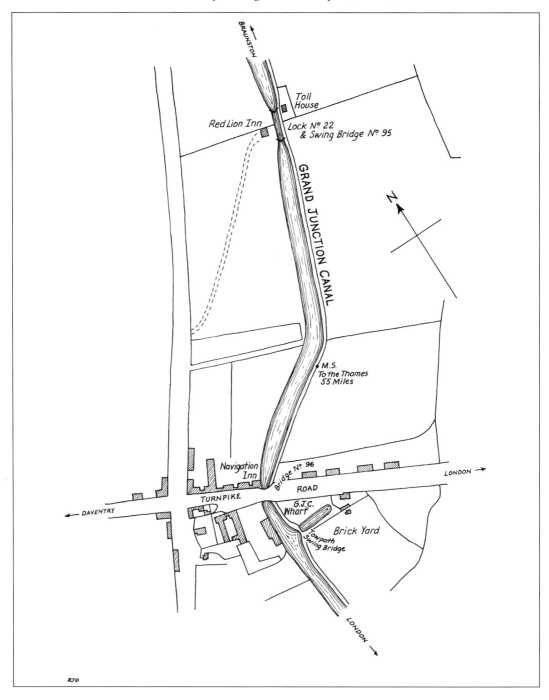

19. Fenny Stratford, Buckinghamshire, 1820

of the barracks at Chatham with their baggage in four waggons. After an overnight stop at Gravesend, they marched into London, being quartered at The Tower for the night. Next day they made their way to Paddington and on the following morning – 25 May – embarked on canal boats for Liverpool. After a stop at Tamworth for a day they reached the port on 3 June. There they boarded *Douglas*, a Liverpool trader, and after a day's voyage landed at Douglas on 5 June. From there they marched to Castletown where they took up their quarters in Rushen Castle.

Unfortunately Major D'Alton was taken ill on arrival in the island, but what was perhaps more serious was the fact that three NCOs and five privates had been too ill to make the journey. Therefore 81 men travelled by canal with a number of wives, plus at least 18 children. The officers, because of their status, each received an additional £1 10s 0d towards meal costs, etc. incurred on the canal journey.[90]

For their return home nine months later, they embarked at Douglas on 9 March, and on arrival at Liverpool found to their dismay that they had to march throughout by road to London. The unit ceased to exist as from 24 March, but most of the men took up residence in Chelsea Hospital.

AID TO THE CIVIL POWER 1826

In 1826, as part of the need to provide additional forces in Lancashire, the Government had agreed at a Cabinet meeting on 30 April to send the 36th Regiment of Foot (Herefordshire) by canal to Manchester. Unfortunately the unit was unable to get to London in time to beat the commencement of the spring stoppage programme, which took place on the canals at this time of year. This normally lasted for between ten days and two weeks and in this period lock repairs/renewals were undertaken and sections of canal were drained to enable men to repair brickwork and also remove silt from the bed of the canal. Spring was chosen as the most suitable time since the level of coal traffic was normally low immediately after the winter, as replenishment orders had not yet percolated

through to the collieries. So this unit had no option but to march throughout by road from Chatham to Manchester. The rearguard, however, consisting of twelve men did manage to travel by canal, as it is recorded that they left Paddington on 7 August for which the carrier charged £8 8s 0d.

General Sir John Byng at Manchester had, however, impressed upon the Government the urgent need to have sufficient forces immediately available to him to deal with any emergency. The delayed arrival of the 36th Regiment of Foot put them in a dilemma. On the one hand there was a need for additional forces in Lancashire, and on the other hand there were no cavalry units surplus to requirements in the country. The military authorities quickly reached a decision following the intervention of the Master General of the Ordnance, the Duke of Wellington, who hastily wrote an order to his artillery commander at Woolwich directing that a troop of Horse Artillery leave straightaway for Manchester by road. Within the space of a few hours Major John Chester's troop, including guns and limbers, left and with commendable dash reached Manchester in the incredibly short time of 46 hours. No sooner had they arrived than Byng sent them to Bolton where he required them to demonstrate to the local populace their fire power capability.

FENNY STRATFORD 1826

The Grand Junction, in its course from London, passes over the Chiltern Hills at Tring in Hertfordshire. The existence of this summit level had, over the years, caused the canal company a lot of trouble and expense as there was considerable difficulty in obtaining an adequate supply of water. The canal company had an uncertain supply from their branch canal to Wendover, supplemented by a few streams which fed into a number of reservoirs adjacent to the waterway. The Grand Junction had found, however, that once Blisworth Tunnel had been opened the volume of water in storage, particularly in a dry season, was barely adequate to lock all traffic over the summit without imposing some form of restriction.

20. Fenny Stratford in 1987 on the Grand Junction Canal alongside Watling Street. This was the loading and unloading point for troops in 1826 when it was not possible to pass over Tring summit due to shortage of water.

To obviate this problem the canal company had driven down a number of deep wells in the area around the reservoirs and installed pumping engines. Even so, on 31 July 1827 the Chairman, Sir Philip Pleydell Bouverie, requested at a committee meeting that 'Waiting-Turns' be instituted immediately, but his plea was rejected.[91]

Another means of saving water at locks was the provision of a sidepond at each lock. This consisted of a brick lined chamber at a level midway between the upper and lower pounds of the canal and communicating with the lock chamber by means of a culvert controlled by a ground paddle. This is known as a 'side-pond paddle'. When a craft enters the full lock and the gates are closed, the side-pond paddle is first raised and the water discharged from the lock into the side-pond until the levels equalize with the lock half empty. The side-pond paddle is then closed and the rest of the water is released from the lock into the lower pound in the

ordinary way. When a boat comes into an empty lock, the side-pond paddle is again the first to be drawn whereupon the water from the side-pond half fills the lock, the remainder being drawn from the upper pound. By this means half a lock of water is saved at each lockage.

In this connection the Chairman reported on 8 August that he had reached agreement with several landowners regarding the purchase of land to enable side-ponds to be constructed at locks 29, 32, 33 and 35, on the west side of Tring summit level situated between Leighton Buzzard and Marsworth. However, by the end of a glorious summer the availability of water to the summit level had reached critical proportions, so much so that when the military authorities wished to move a number of units over this section of canal in the autumn, permission was refused. Instead the terminus on the Grand Junction had to he switched from Paddington to Fenny Stratford in Buckinghamshire at the southern end of an 11¼ mile almost lock-free pound at the point where Watling Street (A5) crosses the canal. John Hassell, in 1819, stated that 'this is a small decayed market town with a church and near it a market house, a sorry little erection.'

However, examination of local Fenny Stratford maps for the period suggests that boats used for troop conveyance would have been loaded and unloaded along the towingpath between Watling Street bridge No. 96 and Fenny Stratford lock No. 22, which has only a rise of one foot, i.e. between 'The Bridge (The Navigation)' and the 'Red Lion' public houses. These establishments were no doubt used by the soldiers before moving on. Boats would have been turned round in the winding hole opposite the swing bridge which gives access to the small Grand Junction basin (70ft x 24ft) alongside Watling Street. The latter would seem to have been the point where regimental baggage was trans-shipped.

To start with, two companies of the 72nd Regiment of Foot (Highland) consisting of eight officers and 238 other ranks under Captain Alexander Logie, left Liverpool early on the morning of 28 September, and by late in the evening of 30 September they had reached Fenny Stratford. From there the 246 men marched on to London to take up their quarters in The Tower.[92]

Just before they arrived, six companies of the 69th Regiment of Foot (South Lancashire) consisting of 32 officers and 709 other ranks under Lt Colonel Sir Charles Cuyler, had left for Mullingar in the county of Westmeath, via Liverpool and Dublin. Like the 72nd they too had to march the road between London and Fenny Stratford, accompanied by 18 waggons loaded with regimental baggage. Loading took place over the period 9 to 13 October.

The earliest boats arriving at Preston Brook were used for the southbound movement of the 61st Regiment of Foot (South Gloucestershire). This unit, consisting of 12 officers, 22 NCOs and 479 other ranks; total 513 men, had originally embarked at Dublin on 10 October, and after leaving their ships at Liverpool on the next day had taken to canal flats for their journey on the Mersey and up the flight of ten locks on the 5¾

mile branch of the Bridgwater Canal from Runcorn to Preston Brook. Presumably the canal flats were used to take the 69th to Liverpool. The 61st left in narrow boats on 13 October and wihin three days had reached Fenny Stratford.[93] Here it was necessary to impress eleven waggons and two carts from Aylesbury for their regimental baggage whilst the regiment marched to Chatham, arriving there on 22 and 23 October.

FLY-BOATS

The canal fly-boat was sleeker and with better lines and thus was able to travel twice as fast as the conventional narrow boat which continued mainly on the coal trade well into the present century. Its width was only 5'10", length was held down to 60' and in consequence when carrying its maximum payload of ten tons it only drew 2'6" of water. The cost was in the order of £160. Fly-boats had absolute priority and paid an additional premium to allow them to travel by night. Slow boats travelling on the canals were required to give precedence to fly-boats by stopping and letting their towline drop into the water; failure to react promptly could result in the sharp knife on the bow of the fly-boat cutting through the towline of the slow boat.

But what was it like to travel by this means of transport – was it slow, easy and comfortable, or was it rough in the extreme? The answer can best be illustrated from the following newspaper cutting:

The journey was made in what was called a long or narrow boat, from the Paddington Basin of the Grand Junction Canal. On an evening late in autumn our family party, consisting of twelve persons embarked on board this vessel, and shortly afterwards we set sail, or rather, I should say, two horses were attached to the towing rope, and after much whistling and shouting we began to move. An experience like this is likely to take firm hold on the mind of a child. I know it did on mine, and many of its details and incidents are firmly impressed on my memory. The voyage was made in delightful autumnal weather, the varied tints of the leaves and the blue of the distant low hills were both sources of the keenest delight to me.

We occupied the middle part of the boat. Our day-room was divided from the sleeping part by means of tarpauling screens. We had a table fixed in the centre, and seats were placed around it. At night a lantern was suspended from the roof of the boat, and light was afforded to us by means of a tallow candle, a dull and mysterious light, as may well be imagined. To me it appeared particularly so, and I well recollect with what awe I sat looking at the depths of the shadow, and expecting every moment to see forms of some kind emerge therefrom. To pass the time the elders of our party played cards, and the young ones amused themselves as well as they could until bedtime. Then we were taken into the next division behind the tarpauling screen to our beds, which were composed of sweet hay, with sheets and blankets upon the top. The gurgle and continuous ripple of the water against the side of the boat, soon lulled us to a sound sleep.

I do not remember at what time we left our beds, but I well recollect that in the dim light of an early November morning we young ones found ourselves on the deck, or rather on the roof of the aftercabin. Tin buckets were dropped into the canal, and were drawn up, dripping, on to the deck, and our ablutions performed. The boat was then momentarily drawn close to the towing-path, and five or six happy mortals leaped on shore and had alternate walks and runs, until the sight of buildings gave us notice that one of the objects of our morning's scamper was about to be attained. These buildings generally turned out to be the stables in which the relays of horses were kept for the service of the boats, and we usually found that provisions, such as butter, cheese, and great round loaves of bread, were to be bought. Our household stores being replenished, and after a short delay, during which horses and men were changed, we renewed our journey to the crack of the whip and whistle of the driver as he urged on his cattle, fresh from the stables and a night's rest, at a smart trot, which, however, did not last long, for the force of habit soon asserted itself, and the two horses dropped down to the steady jog-trot of their predecessors. Still, although the pace was slow, it was continuous. A man stood contemplatively at the rudder; the man with the horses would enliven his spirits with an occasional whistle, and then a snatch or two of a song; and a third man, whom I may perhaps term the mate of our vessel, would make periodic journeys along the ridge of the tarpauling roof of our boat, now and then drop a bucket into the water, draw it up full, dash the water on to the tarpauling, and with the aid of a mop remove the marks of the yesterday's travel.

And so throughout the live-long day we persued our course, through a tolerably level country, with few locks to cause delay or stoppages, except such as drawing up to the side of the canal to let another boat pass, or occasionally to take up some small parcels. I don't remember that we had a single shower of rain during the whole of our voyage. The general run of the scenery has left the idea of the country being generally level, with low, well-wooded hills in the distance; ploughed fields seem to be almost interminable; there were frequent villages and farm-houses, church towers and spires, and many bridges which we passed under with a swish-like noise – these formed a succession of scenes and pictures, the like of which is perhaps not to be seen out of England.

And thus our voyage of four days was accomplished. We arrived safe and sound at about seven o'clock in the evening of November the fifth, 1830, at the Duke's Wharf, Castle Field, Manchester.[94]

In the main troops travelled on Pickford's fly-boats, but there were some instances when Kenworthy's of Manchester also carried them. With regard to volume, the evidence given by John Norton before the House of Commons Select Committee on the Bill for the London – Birmingham railway gives an insight into the sheer volume of fly-boats operating on the canal system. He apparently took a census of craft passing to and from the Grand Junction Canal at Braunston in August 1831, when over a period of 14 days he noted 366 fly-boats. These would have been travelling between London and such points as Birmingham, Wolverhampton, Banbury, Coventry, Stoke-on-Trent and Manchester.

Regimental records show that considerable use was made of this facility, a case in point being revealed by the returns submitted by the 59th Regiment of Foot (2nd Nottinghamshire) wherein it is stated that on 12 August 1830 nine men travelled from the depot at Weedon to Manchester where they picked up the regimental baggage, and on 7 September returned with it to the depot.[95]

Troops being discharged from the army in a strange city in need of finding the canal wharf at which to board a fly-boat home,[96] could easily fall in with the wrong type of person and suffer in consequence. An example of this being Private Robert Bayley, who after ten years in the 91st Regiment of Foot (Argyle & Sutherland Highlanders) was discharged in the White Hart Inn, Chelsea, London, on 11 January 1832. After spending two days with friends he set off to find Pickford's wharf at Paddington to join a boat for Manchester, which was the nearest point by fly-

TABLE 6: *The cost of rail travel in 1831*

BETWEEN WHAT PLACES	AT WHAT PERIODS	AVERAGE DURATION OF THE JOURNEYS OR VOYAGE	RATES OF CONVEYANCE	
			OFFICERS	SOLDIERS ON DUTY AND ALSO DISCHARGED SOLDIERS AND THEIR WIVES
			£ s d	£ s d
Liverpool & Manchester	4 times a day	2 hours	5 0	2 2
Liverpool & Newton	ditto	1 hour	2 0	1 1
Liverpool & Bolton	Twice a day	2 hours	5 0	2 2
Liverpool & Warrington	ditto	1½ hours	2 6	1 6

boat to his home at Rochdale. On his way up Park Lane he met Private Henry Stockwell of the Scots Guards, aged 22. They went into a pub and had a few drinks. On coming out of the pub Stockwell robbed him of a purse containing £1 17s 6d plus a small tin partially filled with tobacco. The assailant ran off and eventually Bayley reported the facts to the Sergeant on duty in the Scots Guards depot at Portman Street barracks. The sergeant, George McIntyre, found Stockwell in his room and searched him. This revealed the missing tobacco tin, but no sign of the purse and its money. Stockwell was arrested and held in custody till his case came up at the Old Bailey on 16 February. Here he was found guilty and six days later the Recorder of London pronounced the 'death penalty'. Although the assailant was a member of the armed forces there is no mention in the army records as to whether Bayley was ever reimbursed.[97]

RAILWAY COMPETITION

With the opening of the Liverpool and Manchester railway in 1826, a new era dawned but it was going to be over a decade before the change became complete. Up to this time whole regiments, more often than not, still marched by road even when canal transport could have been made available, but this new railway linking two important cities went out of its way to secure this additional traffic. Hence almost as soon as it was opened, special arrangements were made

with the War Office under which troops were conveyed between Liverpool and Manchester at 2s 2d each; the amount was arrived at by taking the government allowance of 1s 1d a day, the cost per man when soldiers marched or went by canal, in either case the journey taking two days, against the two hours by rail.

'Women belonging to the Regiment' were carried free so long as there were not more than ten to every 100 men; perhaps those in excess of this proportion travelled with the regimental baggage at eight shillings per ton. These arrangements were made on 30 October 1830, originally to meet any emergency in those days of unrest, and in August 1831 it was agreed to charge the same rates from either Liverpool or Manchester to Bolton.[98] To sum up, therefore, rates for travel by rail were as shown in *table 6*.

The Passenger Tax, introduced in 1832, applied to all persons travelling by coach or rail and brought an ultimatum from the railway company to Lt Colonel John Jordan, Commanding Officer, Liverpool, on 24 October; either the Government remit the tax on military traffic or pay 2/6d per man. The Secretary for War, to whom the matter was referred, agreed to the increase. The revised fare for officers was six shillings.

With the opening of the Warrington and Newton Railway on 25 July 1831, an initially better service was now available to the War Office for troops moving southwards from Liverpool. This new facility was soon put to the test for in September of that year the 21st Regiment of Foot (Royal North British Fusiliers) on returning from their tour of duty in Ireland, travelled by train to Warrington, and instead of using canal transport from Stockton Quay they marched all the way from there to Weedon Depot. The regimental baggage, however, was conveyed throughout by narrow boat from Liverpool to Weedon.

PROPOSED CRAFT FOR TROOP CONVEYANCE 1832

Thomas Grahame, a Glasgow merchant, has been called the last soldier in the struggle to hold the canal system against the overwhelming onslaught of the railways; for ever since 1825 he had been writing books and pamphlets on what the canals should be doing to combat the railways, and among his many proposals was one written to the War Office in July 1832 which is given below:

I beg leave to address you on a matter which I apprehend may lead to a very great saving in the disbursements for the army in Britain and Ireland, by the introduction of an improved, speedy, and cheap mode of conveying troops from one quarter of the country to another, in boats constructed of thin sheet iron, such as are now in use in this neighbourhood, on the Paisley and Ardrossan Canal. These boats, which are fitted each to carry from 80 to 100 passengers, are drawn along the canal by two horses, at the rate of from nine to ten miles an hour. The draft is, in fact, so light, that a boy could draw one of the boats with her complement of passengers, more easily than a horse can draw one of the wooden passage-boats at present in general use on English canals.

In order fully to explain to you the nature of my proposal, I send you enclosed, printed copies of a letter on the subject of these light boats, addressed by me to the Proprietors of Canals on the line of the proposed Birmingham and London Railway; and also, of a short statement, respecting the increased resistance presented to floating bodies, drawn through or along the surface of water at different rates of velocity.

Almost all the great towns and populous districts of England are now connected by inland navigations, either by rivers or canals, and, by a proper use of light iron boats on these navigations. Troops, with their accoutrements and baggage, might be conveyed from one station to another, at a moment's notice, at almost no expense, in an extremely short space of time.

At present, the passage-boats in use on almost all inland navigations, with the exception of those lately introduced on the Paisley Canal, are so heavy and clumsy, as to require a great force to draw them at a very slow rate; but, although the proprietors of all the inland navigations were to introduce the improved light iron passage-boats, this introduction would only be to the extent of supplying the every-day demand for conveyance, and could not, even to this extent, be commanded, except by previous arrangement and notice, and at a considerable expense. To reduce this expense, and at the same time, to render the conveyance available whenever required, even at a moment's notice, it would be necessary that the boats should be provided at the expense, and be entirely at the disposal, of Government.

Were a certain number of these light iron boats kept at or near each of the usual stations of the troops, a whole regiment, with their accoutrements and baggage, might be put on board the requisite number of boats, and four men from each boat being employed with a towing-line, the whole would with perfect ease be conveyed along the navigation at the rate of four miles an hour, and the men being relieved by relays at the end of each hour, or half-hour, the whole regiment might be conveyed a distance of sixty miles without fatigue, between five in the morning and eight at night, and at the end of this journey, all the men would be quite fresh and ready for duty, none of them having laboured so much as an hour during the journey. No other assistance or power would be requisite for moving the boat but the men themselves.

It would be necessary that a certain number of the men should learn to steer the boats, but this would be very easily accomplished, the motion being entirely through still water, unaffected by winds, waves, or tides.

The heavy boats now employed, although proceeding only at the rate of from four to five miles an hour, have so much way or momentum, that, although they would be drawn by men (which is not the case), these men would require to be accustomed to the work, otherwise they would be constantly doing or suffering damage, to or from the bridges or locks, or to the other vessels navigating the canals. But the light boats have so little way or momentum, that they are easily stopped, and are found to do or suffer little or no injury by percussion on the canal works or other vessels. Even at a speed of eight miles an hour, the light boats are found to be quite safe, and neither

FORM, No. 66.

Messrs Pickford & Hoy

COASTWISE OR CANAL.

By Virtue of Authority vested in me by the Right Honorable the Master General and Board of Ordnance, you are hereby required and directed to furnish the under-mentioned Persons with a Conveyance from *London*

to *Liverpool*

Battalion or Corps in which serving, inlisted for, or discharged from	Number	Total Numbers of each to be inserted in words	
1st Batt.n Thos Curry his wife & one child		None	Officers
	One	One pensioner	{ Non-Commissioned { Officers and Men
	One	One	Women
	One	One	{ Children above One { and under Fourteen { Years of Age.

Signature and Rank *W. H. Barton for Superintendent of Shipping absent on Duty*

Station and Date *Royal Arsenal 30 March 1833*

I do hereby certify that the above Persons embarked at

on the   day of   18

and Disembarked at   on the   18

and were accomodated agreeably to the Terms of the Contract,* and that the Baggage conveyed did not exceed the Quantity stationed by the Regulations.

To be signed by the Officer or Non-Commissioned Officer in charge of the Party, and if discharged Men, by them.

{ Signature _____

{ Rank _____

{ Date _____

* Where Provisions are supplied on the Passage, it must be so stated in the Certificate.

500. April, 1832.

21. A Canal Travel Warrant issued in 1833 by the Board of Ordnance at Woolwich for free travel by canal from London.

suffer injury from, nor do injury to the canal, or its locks or bridges, &c.

In this manner troops might be conveyed from London to almost any town or populous district in England in a very short time, and with no outlay or cost other than the tonnages to the canal companies.

In the same way, troops stationed at Dublin, might be conveyed to the interior of Ireland along the Royal and Grand Canals. While, in Scotland, a regiment might with ease pass from Edinburgh to Glasgow, or from one side of the island to the other, in a day.

At present, troops are conveyed from London to Manchester in boats, but these boats are airless and confined, and the time consumed in the passage is long. The boats I propose are roomy, well aired and ventilated, and, at the same time, passengers are perfectly protected from the weather. The form of the boats for carrying troops should not, however, be exactly the same as those on the Paisley Canal. They should be at least eight feet wide, and as long as the locks or the curves on the navigation will admit. A boat of this description, sixty-eight feet in length, would carry ninety, or one hundred passengers and their luggage, and if formed on the principles of the Paisley boats with the recent improvements, might be drawn along an ordinary-sized canal at a rate upwards of four miles an hour, by a force or power not greater than forty pounds. Of course, if formed of a greater length, the pull necessary for the same weight will be diminished, or a greater burden might be carried.

THE PICKFORD'S CONTRACT OF 1832

The Board of Ordnance entered into a three year agreement with Messrs Pickford on 1 February 1832.[95] This document not only set out the charges, but also included a number of interesting details such as the need to give 48 hours notice when a boat was to be specially chartered. Officers were allowed to take 4 cwt of baggage whilst NCOs and other ranks were restricted to 56 lb which included their arms and knapsack. Excess baggage was to be charged at a rate of 6/- per cwt; however, if the boat had been specially chartered, no charge was to be levied.

A boat had to be capable of carrying 40 men, but if officers were accompanying the troops, then 25% of the area had to be allocated to them. Not only was this section to be screened off by a wooden partition or piece of canvas, but it was to include a table plus chair or camp stool. For the troops, clean straw was to be provided. Weather protection was also required, but it was to be provided in such a way as to ensure a free circulation of fresh air. In the fore part of the boat, there was to be a fireplace to enable the men to cook their provisions, and in this connection the officer in charge was permitted to halt the boat to enable the men to purchase same and also carry out toilet functions.

The details of this contract and the service charges levied by railways, packet boats and other canal carriers, etc. in the British Isles, was issued as a printed document on 2 August 1832. The revised update covering canals and packet boats, etc. is to be found in Appendix 'A' towards the end of this book. The canal charges averaged out to approximately 1d per mile in 1833; even the equivalent railway journey in 1839 was still approximately 1d per mile, the latter only appearing cheaper because of the reduced mileage as evidenced from the data given below:

	Canal 1833 miles	Canal 1833 fares	Railway 1839 miles	Railway 1839 fares
London – Coventry	129	10/-	96	7/10d
London – Birmingham	142	12/-	115	9/4d

Journeys by packet boat in Southern Ireland during 1832 were much dearer, averaging out at 1¾d per mile.

It was as well that this work was published, for army accounts had for some time been considerably in arrears and even though payments had been made for services rendered it was not uncommon for questions to be asked long after the event. Take the case of Corporal James Penny who, in 1826 during the depths of winter when the canals were frozen, had to make a journey from Woolwich to Liverpool. Not surprisingly it took him 21 days, but in October 1829 the account was queried and in evidence it was stated that normally, without recourse to canal conveyance, the journey would have taken 16 to 18 days and for marching battalions of the Artillery, 20 or 21 days; so Penny was vindicated. Men from units under the control of the Board of Ordnance were discharged at Woolwich and if possible they were required to travel by canal

TABLE 7 *Analysis of Persons Discharged by Board of Ordnance*

Canal Destination		1830	1831	1832	1833	1834	1835
Birmingham	M	1		1	1		
	F	1					
	C	2			2		
Chesterfield	M		1	1	3		3
	F		1	1	1		3
	C		1				4
Derby	M			1	1	2	4
	F			1	1	1	2
	C			2	4	1	8
Hinckley	M						1
	F						1
	C						3
Leicester	M	1		1	1	6	6
	F	1				5	1
	C	2				13	
Litchfield	M						1
	F						1
	C						2
Liverpool	M	8	14	25	40	44	63
	F	3	10	17	26	29	29
	C	12	25	32	60	58	65
Loughborough	M					1	
	F						
	C						
Macclesfield	M				1	1	2
	F						2
	C					1	2
Manchester	M	5	2	4	7	12	22
	F	3	1	3	5	8	16
	C	3	3	4	19	11	41
Newark	M					1	
	F						
	C						
Northampton	M			1			
	F			1			
	C						

Canal Destination		1830	1831	1832	1833	1834	1835
Nottingham	M	2	1	3		3	11
	F	1		3		2	7
	C	1		12		7	15
Preston Brook	M						2
	F						1
	C						6
Retford	M				1		
	F				1		
	C				2		
Sheffield	M	1		4	6	8	7
	F	1			2	4	6
	C	4			1	9	1
Stockport	M			1		1	1
	F					1	1
	C						2
Stockton Quay	M	1	2				
	F		2				
	C						
Stoke-on-Trent	M	1	2	3		2	4
	F	1	1	3		2	3
	C	3	4	10		2	9
Stone (Staffs)	M	1					1
	F						1
	C						2
Warwick	M					1	
	F						
	C						
Whitchurch (Salop)	M					1	
	F					1	
	C					1	
Wolverhampton	M		4			1	4
	F		2			1	2
	C		12			4	
TOTALS		59	88	134	185	245	370

M=Male   F=Female   C=Children

TABLE 8: *The number of Artillery recruits travelling from Ireland to London in the 1830s.*

	Ex Northern Ireland via Newry/WarrenPoint thence by steamship to Liverpool and on by canal to London	Ex Southern Ireland by canal to Dublin thence by steamship round England to London
1834	57	3
1835	32	6
1836	33	11
1837	74	86
1838	271	116
1839	Nil	54
1840	Nil	86

boat together with their wives and children. Travel warrants were issued to cover their movements, which had to be completed by the carrier as well as the person conveyed. To give an indication of the extent of movement made by canal from London, an analysis has been taken for the six years ended 1835 and this is given in *table 7.*

For many the journey home did not finish in the town at which they got off the fly-boat. Indeed for some there was still a long way to walk, such as from Manchester to Bury, Chorley or Rochdale which may not have seemed far, but journeys from Stone in Staffordshire to Shrewsbury or from Chesterfield in Derbyshire to Bradford must have been very different. With little or no protection from the elements and very little money the journey must indeed have been very hard, especially on small children.[99]

JOURNEYS END 1834–1844

Surprisingly a large proportion of the recruits for the Artillery came from Ireland, both from the North as well as from the South. For these young men a journey by sea was perhaps quite an experience, especially if gales were encountered on the Irish Sea. To reach Dublin some travelled by canal before joining a

steamship for London, whilst those from the North would have landed at Liverpool where there was the prospect of a long journey by canal fly-boat to London. From London, all recruits would have had to make their way to the barracks at Woolwich, a distance of approximately eight miles – a nice one day's march.

The number who travelled by canal up to the end of 1840 are listed in *table 8.*

Not only was 1838 the high spot for travel by canal, but it also heralded several changes. Firstly, as from 12 February, a steamer was used for journeys from Kilrush in County Clare up the Shannon Estuary to Limerick before joining the canal boat for the trip across Ireland to Dublin. Secondly, the last recorded journey from Ulster, involving movement by canal in England, took place on 24 July. Rail travel from Liverpool to London was first used as from 28 January 1839.[100]

Travel through England's green and pleasant land by canal boat must have seemed to the poor an enjoyable form of transport, albeit a little slow perhaps, but it had the benefit of saving one's shoe leather. It is therefore pleasing to record that of all the journeys undertaken by these Irish recruits there was only one which became unpleasant in the extreme. This concerns 15 recruits for the 4th Battalion of Royal Artillery who set out from Ulster in the New Year of 1838, and following a rough trip across the Irish Sea eventually reached Liverpool where on 6 January they joined a narrow boat for the through journey to Paddington. As they left the temperature started to drop and no doubt they huddled around the stove to get what heat they could. Through cold and dank tunnels and on over canals which were only being kept open by exertion of the ice-breaker crews, till at last, on 12 January, they reached Braunston. Here they found, much to their chagrin, that the Grand Junction Canal had succumbed to 'jack-frost' and was totally closed to all traffic.

Luckily for these recruits, who by now were many miles away from any place they knew, there was with them William Malley, a Colour Sergeant-Major from the 9th Battalion who no doubt, because of his lengthy service, was well aware of what actions he should take to ensure that these recruits should reach Woolwich safely within the regulations laid down under the Mutiny Act. He soon got them together, and with their limited amount of baggage set off along Watling Street to London where they may have been lucky enough to find a boat owner willing to take them down the Thames to their destination. Since they would have stopped at night, the journey time of seven days when one considers the conditions under foot, was very commendable (which perhaps shows what could be done when you have the right person in charge of the detachment).

Conversely, pensioners suffered the same fate, an example being Driver Thomas Coleman, who after his discharge from the Royal Artillery, made his way from Woolwich to London only to find that the canal was frozen over. As he held a warrant for travel by canal and he had no marching money, he made his way back to Woolwich where he pleaded his case. The matter was discussed at the Board meeting in their Pall Mall offices and approval was given for him to be paid marching money for the distance, plus a daily allowance to cover the period between his discharge and the receiving of his marching money.[101]

The level of business for troop movement undertaken by Messrs Pickford for units coming under the Board of Ordnance during the final years till the canals ceased to be used, is shown in *table 9*.[102]

Whilst it has not been possible to determine the level of out-payments for the movement of troops covering all aspects of the British Army at this period, as a guide it is worth noting that the strength of infantry regiments of foot stationed in England and Wales during 1838 was approximately 18 times larger than those coming under the jurisdiction of the Board of Ordnance. Detailed examination of the Ordnance records show that a number of men made journeys off the normal London – Liverpool run. In 1841 there were movements from London to Leicester and Nottingham as well as an interesting one from Wolverhampton to Welshpool for which Pickfords charged 12/-. Thereafter movement was restricted to the London – Liverpool run, despite the existence of railways linking the two

TABLE 9: *Troop movements carried by Pickfords from London to Liverpool, 1834–1844*

Year	Payment	Equivalent Journeys London – Liverpool
1834	£326 6 0	408
1835	149 13 0	187
1836	174 18 0	219
1838	418 17 0	523
1839	233 1 0	291
1840	41 9 0	52
1841	21 4 0	27
1842	15 10 0	19
1843	5 18 0	7
1844	2 14 0	3

cities, culminating in the last known canal journeys in 1844. These involved a private from the 3rd Battalion who left London on 27 February, with his wife and child for Liverpool; and Private W. Redfern of the 6th Battalion who travelled from City Road Basin in London to Manchester on 9 July. Little did he know as he sat in the boat with the horses galloping ahead under a summer's sky, that his passage was to mark the end of an epoch.

CONCLUSION

In the preceding chapters, a survey has been made of the special role played by the canals over a short period of England's history. Two themes are apparent, security and speed.

During this period, the country was under the stresses, first, from war overseas, and, later, fear of industrial unrest that might lead to nation-wide revolution. Regimental records make only casual references to the details of troop movements across the country: indeed, 'marched' was the word used for at least one transit by canal. This promotes the idea that canal travel was routine for the military on the move.

Another aspect of security was revealed by the Member of Parliament who told his colleagues that he saw the army on the move as 'an encroaching thing'. It is clear that the legislators were concerned to shield the citizens from the military as much to protect the soldiers from the temptations of city life. On both these counts, conveyance by canal fitted the bill.

Furthermore, the speed and economy of the canals appealed to the War Office. Once the burdens of war were removed the government acceded to the demands of economy. Pay-cuts were imposed in all departments. On the canals, for troops, their families and their equipment 'marching money' was paid for the estimated number of days required for the journey to be undertaken.

On the canals, the transit time between London and Liverpool was reduced from 14 days on the roads to 4½ or 5 days to the great satisfaction of the custodians of HM Treasury. However, these calls on the canals fell away remorselessly in the 1830's under the combined influence of improved road construction and the introduction of steam both at sea and on the new railways. Surprisingly, emergency arrangements for travel by canal continued in successive Mutiny Acts until 1871. Comparable requirements do not seem to have been laid on the railways in their formative years.

All in all, the canals showed what they were capable of when arrangements worked satisfactorily, but there were times when water shortage, ice and spring closures wrought havoc. Surprisingly the use of river navigation appears to have been kept to the absolute minimum, perhaps due to problems encountered when moving against the flow coupled with the fact that the dimensions of most barges made them unsuitable for service off the canals.

The canal carriers, apart from early problems with supply and fitments, provided as good a service as they were able having regard to the conditions under which they operated. However, in the post-Waterloo period when canal traffic of all kinds was on the increase, those in Horse Guards often had to undertake delicate negotiations so that the price was right and the agreed time of movement fitted in well with the anticipated low level of commercial traffic.

Lord steer my sheltered barge along
Clear off the banks of sin
Clear off the world's reproaching throng
And bring me safely in.

Let me Thy holy word esteem
And to the Lord be given
And tow me up the blissful stream
Into the dock of Heaven.

Two verses of a Hymn from the *Canal Boatmen's Magazine 1829*

CHAPTER FIVE

Troops on the Royal Military Canal

IN 1803 Napoleon was at war with the United Kingdom. As part of this conflict the French had been concentrating most of their effort on preparing a scheme for the invasion of this island. To this end, troops had been quartered at points on the coast between Ostend and Boulogne, the idea being to transfer this large army in barges, etc., across the English Channel under ideal weather conditions as a surprise move similar to that proposed by the Germans in 1940.

From this threat stemmed the proposal, in 1804, to build a canal from Shorncliffe, east of Hythe in Kent, round Romney Marsh to join the Eastern Rother at Iden just above Rye in East Sussex, which became known as the Royal Military Canal. There is another part of this canal from the river Brede at Winchelsea to Cliff End, but so far no evidence to suggest that this part of the canal was ever used for conveying troops other than those maintaining it.

The drawing up of this scheme was the brain-child of Lt Colonel Brown of the Royal Staff Corps (Royal Engineers). When General Sir David Dundas, GOC Southern District, who was responsible for co-ordinating the defence of Britain, saw Brown's report he commented:

This scheme would not be totally unproductive and be of use for commerce and husbandry purposes. Floating defences would be manageable and contribute much of its strength and the quick movement of troops.

Brown's report together with the GOC's comments, were forwarded on 18 September 1804 to Frederick, Duke of York, the Commander-in-Chief, who very shortly afterwards sent them to the Secretary of State, Lord Camden, with the added observation:

In regard to the proposal for cutting a canal betwixt Hythe and the river Rother, for the purpose of military defence, by separating an enemy landed upon the coast of Romney Marsh from the interior of the country, I am to press this measure most earnestly upon the consideration of H.M. Government.

The Duke of York, however, was so keen on the project that he had already obtained the authority to start work immediately from William Pitt, who had become Prime Minister again as from 7 May of that year. In addition, Pitt also held the post of Lord Warden of the Cinque Ports from 1792 till his death on 23 January 1806. Work was soon put in hand under the direction of Major General Brownrigg, Quarter-master General, and by the summer of 1806 was sufficiently far advanced to warrant an inspection by the Duke of York.

On 23 June 1806, the Royal Waggon Train (Royal Corps of Transport) was instructed to move a waggon from their depot in Mitcham Road, Croydon, to London and there collect a boat and take it to Hythe for use on the canal. During August, the Duke inspected various army units at Canterbury, Dover, Folkestone and Shorncliffe, held in readiness to defeat an invasion from France. On the morning of Sunday, 11 August, he boarded a boat at Shorncliffe, about half a mile from the barracks, together with his attendants, and was hauled by horses of the Royal Waggon Train from there to the site of Iden Lock, a distance of just over 19½

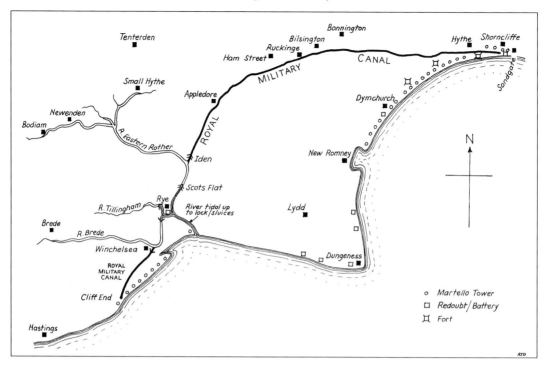

22. The Royal Military Canal in Romney Marsh, 1820

miles, in 2¾ hours. Horses were changed at Warehorne, about half way along the canal where the Royal Waggon Train had a detachment for this purpose. He was unable to proceed further by boat, as work on Iden Lock had not yet commenced; so he had to continue his tour via Battle, Hastings, Eastbourne and Lewes, to Brighton by other means.

Initially the task of building the canal had been entrusted to contractors, but their work fell far short of expectations. Therefore the military authorities put soldiers to work on the canal with a twofold purpose, firstly to construct the canal and secondly to be on hand in the event of the invasion taking place.

By September 1808 there was still a lot to be done under the direct supervision of the Royal Staff Corps, who had 190 men stationed at Hythe with a further 26 at Winchelsea. Whilst these men carried out the specialists' tasks such as bridge and culvert construction, the labouring work was done by the 778 men of the South

Lincolnshire Militia and 225 men of the Pembroke Militia. The dimensions of the canal were quite large by the standards normally adopted at that period. The surface width was 62ft with a bottom width of 26ft, but the depth of 9ft was exceptional.[103] This, of course, was to prevent the enemy from fording the canal.

Early in 1809, the military road between Rye and Strand Bridge Winchelsea had been completed, reducing the distance between these two points by 1½ miles. This was just as well, because the canal made it possible to move troops between Rye and Shorncliffe in one day as compared with two days when marching over the country roads via Dymchurch. Indeed Brownrigg reported in April that:

If extraordinary expedition is at any time required, troops from Dover can now reach Hastings or Battle (distance of over 40 miles) in one day.

No doubt the 150 officers and 2,800 other ranks, who could be stationed at Shorncliffe barracks, would have been the first to travel in the event of the invasion alarm being raised. Movement to/from Rye was possible, but the existence of Scots Flat (Float) sluice just over one mile down the Rother from the lock, marked the commencement of the tidal part of the river. Naturally this part of the river was only occasionally used for troop movement when proceeding to/from ships in the harbour or Winchelsea. In the latter event, movement over the tidal waters of 2¼ miles would have involved the Eastern Rother as well as the Rock Channel on the river Tillingham to the junction with the river Brede where the lock lies underneath the walls of Martello tower No.30 in Rye. Thereafter there follows a 2 mile stretch of river navigation to Strand Bridge.

Soldiers on the march sooner or later require refreshment and what better place to go to than a public house? For those working along the canal there sprang up 'The Carpenters Arms' in St Mary's Road by West Hythe Bridge, and the 'Blue Anchor' at Ruckinge. But these could only be seen and not used by those travelling on the barges, which must have been very frustrating. Therefore it is not surprising to find that the terminal points were well provided; in Hythe there still stands near the site of the Royal Waggon Train barracks, 'The Duke's Head' by the bridge of the same name.

At Iden on the other side of the road from the Rother there stood 'The Ordnance'.[104] The one and only landlord of this establishment, Stephen Ward, apparently in 1806 added a room to his cottage, which was on government land, without seeking their permission. As soon as general troop movement ceased, he shut up shop and went off to the wars where he lost an arm. When he returned he discovered that he was not to receive a pension for his disablement, so he did what he could by gardening. Eventually he decided to come clean with the authorities over his situation. The Board of Ordnance, being sympathetic to his circumstances, granted him a lease of the ground for 21 years at £1 per annum.

Down the Rother at Scots Flat, there stood 'The Star' which lasted long after troop conveyance had ceased, being still shown on the 1921 1" os Map. Today the building still stands,

23. General Sir David Dundas (1735–1820) who as GOC Southern District foresaw that the construction of the Royal Military Canal would provide for quick movement of troops.

but is a private house. Below the walls of the ancient town of Winchelsea, at the junction of the Royal Military Canal and the river Brede, there stands the 'Bridge Inn' which has been on this site since 1586. During the period 1775–1855 it was known as the 'Bridge House' and besides being a useful hostelry for the troops prior to their march up the steep hill to their barracks in the town, it was also for a time a toll office. Today, although enlarged, it still has relics of its long past.

Iden Lock on the canal, when erected in September 1808, was capable of passing boats 72ft long by 16ft beam, drawing five feet of water. It had the unusual feature of an additional pair of gates at the river end to permit craft to enter the canal when the river was in flood. Scots Float Lock, at the tidal limit of the Rother, was a truly massive affair; not only had it to contend with the floodwater, but also hold back several miles of water whilst the tide was out. It is therefore not surprising that there was great reluctance on the part of the military to allow their craft to pass through this lock, for each of the four gates measured 9'3" wide by 24'6" high.

24. Badge of the Royal Staff Corps who provided the qualified staff for building and maintaining the Royal Military Canal between 1805 and 1838.

THE NAPOLEONIC SCENE 1809–1815

The Peninsular War reached a climax in November 1808 when Napoleon entered Spain and drove the patriotic, but ill-commanded and undisciplined, Spanish troops before him. Sir John Moore rushed to their assistance, but was unable to stem the tide and had to fight a rearguard action at Corunna on 16 January 1809, to protect the withdrawal of his men. When the survivors eventually reached England they were in a poor shape, but no matter where they disembarked they still had to march to their appointed station, ready to meet the expected invasion from France.

Just when it seemed the canal was about to come into prominence for troop conveyance, the weather took a hand. On 30 January 1809, when there was a high spring tide coupled with a severe storm, the sea breached the canal bank at Shorncliffe, but luckily the damage was not great and therefore was soon repaired. However, the break in the Sandgate – Shorncliffe road was far more serious and took several days to rectify.[105]

To move the barges on the canal, the Royal Waggon Train had a detachment of troops stationed at Hythe, made up of: two officers, one quarter-master, 13 NCOs and 70 other ranks, with 50 horses. As far as is known the first troops to travel on the canal were 21 men from the 1st Battalion of the 95th (Rifle Brigade); these had left Brighton on 7 February under orders to proceed to Shorncliffe, and were instructed by Lt Colonel John Brown, Commandant Royal Staff Corps, to complete their journey by barge from Iden Lock on 10 February 1809. Next day the main part of the Regiment consisting of 301 men, followed. The benefit of travel in barges hauled by horses of the Royal Waggon Train, even though for only a short part of their journey, must have been a tremendous relief to these exhausted troops; for when W.H.Cope wrote their Regimental history towards the end of the last century he remarked that :

The condition of the survivors and the unwounded was deplorable. The appearance of the Battalion was squalid and miserable. Most of the men had lost their appointments (equipment); many were without shoes; and their clothing was not only tattered and in rags,

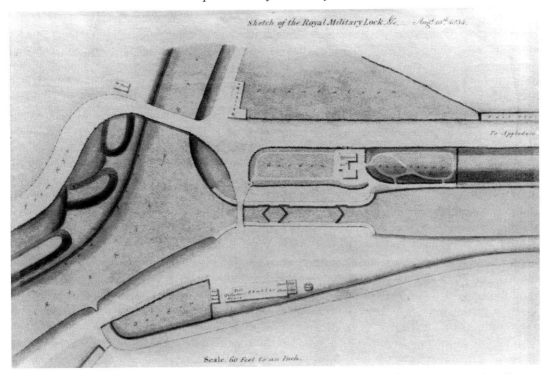

25. Iden Lock, 1834, on the Royal Military Canal at the junction with the Eastern Rother showing barracks, toll office and on the left the remains of Mr Ward's inn (Ordnance Arms). This lock was completed in September 1808 by the Royal Staff Corps and has a second set of gates for use when the river is in flood.

but in such a state of filth and so infested with vermin, that on new clothing being served out, it was burnt at the back of the barracks.

No sooner had these men been safely disembarked at Hythe than orders were received to convey seven officers and 269 other ranks of the 1st Battalion 36th (Herefordshire) from there to Rye on their way from Dover to Battle. Two days later one officer and 88 other ranks of the 1st Battalion 82nd (Prince of Wales) travelled by barge en route from Dover to Lewes.

By now the staff and horses of the Royal Waggon Train must have been put on their mettle since orders came in the space of five days in that February to move the 36th back along the canal, together with the 81st (Loyal North Lancashire), and on the following day a further part of the 82nd.

Some idea of the difficulties of keeping formations together when embarking under fire, can be gained from the composition of the undermentioned party which next passed along the canal. They had come from Corunna, disembarked at Portsmouth and then marched along the coast to Rye.

Guards – various	5
6th Regt (Warwickshire)	2
9th Regt (East Norfolk)	69
30th Regt (Cambridgeshire)	2
42nd Regt (Royal Highland)	8
50th Regt (West Kent)	6
52nd Regt (Oxfordshire)	9
71st Regt (Highland)	3
91st Regt (Princess Louise)	7
95th Regt (Rifle Brigade)	6
Total	117 men

Next month a similar movement took place, when one officer and 56 other ranks on their

26. Artist's impression of the Royal Waggon Train moving a barge loaded with a company of the 95th Foot (Rifle Brigade) from Iden to their barracks at Shorncliffe on the Royal Military Canal in 1809.

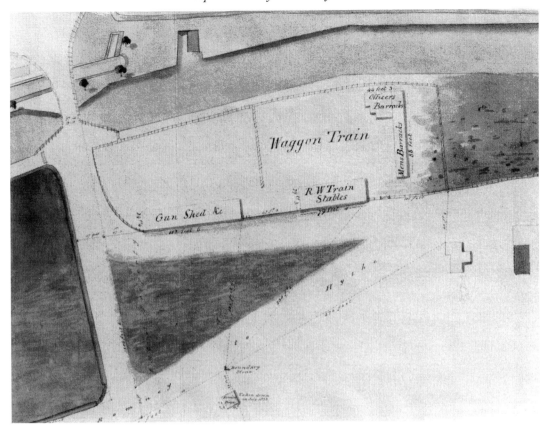

27. Hythe, 1834, showing the layout of the Royal Waggon Train depot beside the Royal Military Canal. Opposite is the dock of the Royal Staff Corps with its boathouse for the Commissioner's barge used on canal inspection.

march from Margate to Lewes, passed along the canal. This time the personnel came from the following regiments: 5th, 23rd, 81st, 82nd and King's German Legion. (The latter unit was raised in 1803 under a Royal Warrant and consisted mainly of Hanoverians.) The men in this move formed part of the new army being gathered together to fight the French in the Peninsula.

April saw another detachment of the King's German Legion making use of the canal on their way from Ramsgate to Bexhill, and these were closely followed by 30 men from the 36th with their officers dressed in a grey top coat kept together with a red sash, proceeding from Ramsgate to Battle.

Movement was not all one way as Militia units (men recruited for service within any part of Great Britain) were sent in to replace regiments of the line, who were required for overseas service. The first of these units to travel by the canal in this part of England was the Montgomery Militia. Ever since the early days of 1808 they had been trudging along the roads through southern England under their Commandant, Lt Colonel Thomas Browne, staying at various towns and villages before arriving at the old Silverhill barracks in the spring of 1809. These barracks, about halfway between Roberts-bridge and Hurst Green, were on elevated ground with extensive views across the Sussex countryside.

28. Hythe, 1806, showing the Royal Military Canal with Scanlons Bridge in the foreground which had to be dismantled in the event of invasion.

To this place came a letter from Horse Guards, written on 24 May, instructing the unit to march to Rye and then on 30 May to travel by barge along the Royal Military Canal to Hythe. But although this sounds straightforward, difficulties soon appeared.

Firstly, it was discovered that the sea port of Rye some 16 miles away could not accommodate all the men, so arrangements were made for the company, under Captain John Dickin, to go to Winchelsea instead. Four waggons having been impressed on 28 May to convey the militia's baggage, etc., the first drum beat was at 4.30 to raise the sleeping men, and at 5 am they marched out of the barracks along the turnpike road. After a march of 3 miles they reached Bodyham (Bodiam) bridge which was the limit of navigation on the Eastern Rother. Now it would have been feasible for barges to have been made available at this point for the conveyance of the baggage direct to Hythe, but the military in this area never made use of civilian craft and furthermore those operated by the Royal Waggon Train only worked along the line of defensive waterways since they might be required at short notice for troop conveyance in the event of an invasion taking place. So on they went, and at Staple Cross the company for Winchelsea parted from the rest and made their way via Broad Oak and Udymer (Udimore). The three companies, under Captains Edward Lloyd, Robert John Harrison and William Philip Daykin, continued on via Beckley to Rye. Next day the three companies marched out of the town up the military road to Scots Flat sluice where the assembled military barges were first loaded with the baggage and then with the men, including those who had marched the 5¼ miles from Winchelsea. All in all there were 234 men plus 18 officers. The men perhaps thought that, like other regiments who had used this type of conveyance before, they would be taken all the way to Hythe; but the authorities had other ideas in mind, for after a journey of only 4½ miles they had to disembark at Appledore Bridge and then march 2½ miles to Reading Street. Here they stayed till 11 August when they marched to New Romney and after an overnight stay moved on to Hythe where they found fresh instructions

ordering them on to Dover on the following day. This short barge-working was no doubt convenient to the Royal Waggon Train, since on the next day the 122 men of the Radnor Militia, who had marched from Bexhill to Scots Flat sluice under Captain John Meredith, were conveyed along the canal to Hythe. From there they marched out to help man the Martello Towers between Hythe and Dungeness.

On 8, 10, and 13 June the 852 men of the Shropshire Militia under Colonel Lord Bradford, enjoyed the delights of being moved along the canal in barges, with the Buckinghamshire Militia from Eastbourne doing the same on 7, 9, and 10 June. The latter move was spread over three days as 21 officers, 74 NCOs, 2 drummers and 506 other ranks were involved. Their presence in the area allowed two companies from 2nd Battalion of the 95th, in their dark green uniforms, to pass along the canal to Rye on 30 June together with one company of the Royal Staff Corps, on their way to Portsmouth to board ships for the Peninsula.

The 1,317 men of the King's German Legion, dressed in their red tunics and grey trousers, arrived from Battle and passed along the canal to Shorncliffe; the 1st Battalion on 5 and 6 July with the 2nd Battalion on the following two days, on their way to take part in an expedition to Antwerp, in the hope that if it succeeded it would compel Napoleon, who was struggling on the Danube, to recall part of his army.

The expedition, under Lord Chatham, eventually sailed on 28 July but only succeeded in capturing Flushing. The troops were left on the low island of Walcheren, where a fever broke out which swept away thousands and so weakened the constitutions of those who recovered that few were fit for active service again. It was not surprising, therefore, that orders for movement issued on 29 November were couched in the following terms – 'those able to march'.

4 December heralded the departure of the 1st and 2nd Battalions of the 50th (West Kent), in their red tunics and light brown trousers, consisting of five officers and 285 other ranks under Lt Colonel G. Walker, from Shorncliffe to Silverhill. In view of the condition of the men, it

is not surprising that the baggage was left at Iden Lock for onward movement by waggon, whilst the men continued on down the Rother, through Rye to Winchelsea, before marching on to their destination. Next day came the 1st Battalion of the 36th by the same route to Battle. Lastly came survivors of the 1st and 2nd Battalions of the King's German Legion proceeding to Bexhill.

At this date, if required, the Royal Waggon Train could move 800 men in one day in the twenty barges which they had on the canal.[106] Generally, each barge was hauled by three horses and could complete the passage of just over 20 miles from Shorncliffe to Scots Float Sluice in about four hours. This was quite an achievement, since none of the eighteen bridges through which the barges had to pass had a towing path underneath and in consequence the towline had to be detached and reaffixed at each one. In addition, steering had to be done with great care as the canal had been built in straight reaches with 90 degree turns every 500ft so that each reach could be commanded by a battery.

So between bridges, the barges must have averaged 6 mph.

Following what must have seemed a successful year, Colonel Brown was able to state in his report on the canal to the Commissioners in 1810, that:

The conveyance of Troops by the Military Canal has been very frequent, and all the Corps passing Coastways have been so conveyed, and although the saving to the Public cannot be introduced into the Accounts of the Canal, it is, nevertheless very considerable; two days march being converted into one.

Barracks for the Royal Staff Corps had been started at Hythe in 1808, but four months before their completion Captain F. Leicester and 55 others were ordered away to Portsmouth, leaving by canal on 26 February 1810, accompanied by three companies from the 2nd Battalion of the 95th, all destined for the Peninsula. Other elements of the 95th eventually left during March after some doubts as to whether the icing conditions on the canal would mean that they would have to march throughout by road. One company of the 95th, however, was taken to Rye

29. Hythe *c.*1905 showing the rebuilt Scanlons Bridge with a barge that used to trade on the Royal Military Canal by the overgrown entrance to the Royal Staff Corps dock.

by barge from Shorncliffe, whilst parliamentary elections were taking place at Hythe, returning by the same means after a stay of only three days. Four days later, after having loaded all their baggage onto barges, they left by canal en route for Portsmouth for service in Portugal.

Redeployments for this move had been completed earlier, when the 796 men of the 3rd Lancashire Militia under Colonel Wilson Braddyll had been transported by canal on their way from Lewes to Dover, in May, followed ten days later by the 124 men of the Caernarvon Militia under Captain Thomas Jones, who proceeded by barges as far as Winchelsea before marching on to Chichester.

On 26 November, the baggage belonging to the 1st Battalion of the 52nd (Oxfordshire) who were serving in Spain, was moved along the canal to Scots Flat by a small party of twenty men, under Sergeant James Meresh, in their red tunics and grey trousers on their way from Deal to Battle.

Napoleon was now at the height of his powers, for in July 1810 he had annexed Holland and by December had added the coast of Germany as far as Hamburg. The danger of invasion was therefore still very real so regiments were redeployed to frustrate an enemy landing.

At the beginning of December, over three days, the 750 men of the 2nd Battalion of 52nd, used the canal on their journey from Deal to Lewes, followed on 4 and 5 December by 460 men of the 2nd Battalion of 35th (Sussex), who travelled on the waters of the canal from Iden Lock when marching from Chichester to Shorncliffe, where they were being assembled with a view to participating in another invasion of Holland.

There was no winding hole by Iden Lock for barges on the canal in which to turn, so empty barges from Hythe had to lock out into the river and turn with the aid of the current and then lock up into the canal before embarking troops and their baggage.

Wellington still had insufficient troops in Portugal to stem the French in the open fields, so reinforcements were gathered together and despatched. On 19 January 1811, the first part the 71st (Highland), consisting of three companies,

left Dover for Portsmouth. The marching orders provided for an additional day being taken in the event of the canal being frozen, but as circumstances turned out this was not necessary. The sight of Highland troops in their kilts sitting on the four lines of benches in the barges, must have been quite a spectacle, but from the troops' angle there was no cover for them so no doubt they had trouble keeping warm.

The rest of the Battalion was slow to follow; the major part of the 1st and 2nd Battalions did not move along the canal till 3 June, with the rearguard consisting of 100 men not travelling until 5 July. These men had been replaced by the Anglesey Militia, consisting of 135 men under Lt Colonel William Hughes, who had travelled to Rye by canal on 8 June from Shorncliffe, after marching from Canterbury. In order to make better use of the militia forces available, it was decided, in 1811, to move from Ireland to England certain regiments and in return replace them with English or Welsh units. As part of this arrangement 149 men of the Caernarvon Militia under Captain Richard Jones, together with 22 women and 20 children, marched from Worthing to Dover which involved them, once again, travelling by this canal; but this time from Scots Flat to Shorncliffe. On 9 August they left Dover aboard the *Thetis* and eventually reached Monkstown, just outside Cork, on 23 August.

Generally cavalry units would have been expected to ride their horses between locations, but occasionally circumstances warranted them being dismounted. This situation pertained early in August as a result of certain units being severely mauled in Spain with heavy losses of horses, and as a result being shipped home. The first to travel on this canal were 108 men of the 4th Dragoon Guards (Royal Irish) whilst escorting their baggage from Shoreham to Canterbury. Next day 39 dismounted men of the 3rd Dragoon Guards (Prince of Wales) followed on the canal whilst on their march from Eastbourne to Canterbury. No doubt they found travel by canal a welcome relief, since their riding-boots were not suitable for foot-slogging.

On 23 March, the Royal Manx Fencibles were disbanded in the Isle of Man and shortly afterwards some of these discharged soldiers joined with some of the inhabitants in a riot at Ramsey. Order was eventually restored by the Manx Volunteer Cavalry, but nevertheless the Lieutenant-Governor, the Hon. Cornelius Smelt, felt justified in asking the Secretary of State to provide some regular forces to maintain law and order and also to assist the Revenue officers as necessary. The Secretary of State replied on 6 April to the effect that a unit was under orders to proceed to the island, but by 3 May the Governor had heard nothing further so reiterated his request. Eventually, on 17 August, orders were despatched from Horse Guards to the 11th Royal Veteran Battalion then stationed at Winchelsea, to the effect that the men were to be inspected on 20 August and on the next day to travel by the canal to Hythe.

However, it appears that there was some confusion, possibly not enough serviceable barges were available, for on 19th the instruction was cancelled. A 'stop/go' situation appears to have arisen, for only two days later orders were issued to the effect that they were to use the canal on the march to Dover. On 24 August, Captain William Thomas Tayler, who was in charge of the 331 men, was only able to find enough barges to carry 109 men from Scots Flat. The major portion therefore marched throughout by road, and after a long sea journey eventually reached Douglas where nine men reported sick, the remainder taking up their garrison duties at Ramsey, Peel, Castletown, as well as Douglas. The unit was destined to stay there for at least another three years.

22 November saw a composite move, when the undermentioned, who had assembled at Shorncliffe on the previous day, first travelled by barge before marching on to Portsmouth where they were to embark on ships bound for Portugal to help Wellington stem the French advance.

9th Regt (East Norfolk)	50	
31st Regt (Huntingdonshire)	20	
51st Regt (2nd Yorkshire)	50	
52nd Regt (Oxfordshire)	30	
60th Regt (Royal American)	20	
95th Regt (Rifle Brigade)	52	
	Total	222 men

Out in the Peninsula things had not been going well for the 1st Battalion of 3rd Regiment of Foot (Buffs), who had not only suffered a number of casualties, but had many men missing, presumably prisoners of the French. Therefore the 2nd Battalion, who were in barracks at Deal and up to strength following an intake of Militiamen, were ordered to send out replacements.

Accordingly on 27 February 1812, 157 other ranks under the command of Captain Charles Ramus Forrest, assisted by Ensign John Simpson Hughes, made their way to Shorncliffe where they boarded barges for Scots Flat. On arrival they marched on to Portsmouth where, on 7 March, they boarded the Transport *Briton* for a lengthy sea voyage which lasted until 2 April.

At the same time three men from the 9th (East Norfolk) assembled at Shorncliffe and passed along the canal on their way to Chichester, together with recruits for the King's German Legion who had recently arrived at Dover en route to Bexhill. In addition, on 30 June approximately, 100 men from the 1st Battalion, King's German Legion, arrived by sea at Dover from Plymouth and made their way to Bexhill in the same manner as the recruits. On 11 April a sergeant and 70 other ranks from the 2nd Battalion of the 3rd, marched from Dover to Shorncliffe. There they boarded a barge for Scots Flat and afterwards marched on to Portsmouth.

Following Sweden's decision to join forces with Napoleon in 1809, the Admiralty mounted a campaign later that year which resulted in the capture of the small island of Anholt, in the Kattegat between Sweden and Denmark. The island was then used as a point at which the British fleet in the Baltic could obtain water supplies as well as providing a refuge for our ships trading with Russia.

Initially it was garrisoned by a small number of Royal Marines, but in 1812 a high level decision was taken that the defence of the island should in future be undertaken by the military, releasing the naval personnel for their normal duties. As all regiments of the line were fully committed the only course open to Horse Guards, now that Napoleon had invaded Russia in June, was to withdraw some of the older soldiers from the south east part of England.

Accordingly, on 29 July orders were issued for the 323 men of the 11th Veteran Battalion, under Captain Leonard K. Willard, to march from their barracks at Winchelsea, together with their baggage which occupied twelve waggons to Iden Lock where they were to board barges for Shorncliffe, and from there to march on to Dover. At that port they were to board *HMS Dover*, but the Admiralty transport department had advised the Army authorities that the ship would not accommodate them all, and furthermore, that no other vessel could be provided. The result was that Lieutenant Thomas Phillips had to return with 32 men and four waggon loads of baggage on 13 September by the same route. No doubt one barge was sufficient for the detachment. The three companies stayed at Fort York on the island till September 1814, when they returned to England and took up residence at Greenwich.

Early in 1813, a detachment of the Royal Waggon Train under Captain Charles Turner, was detailed to work the canal; it consisted of three other officers, six NCOs, one trumpeter and 85 other ranks. With them were 100 horses and 21 waggons. They seem to have had a relatively easy time for records suggest that there were no troop movements along the canal till 3 May, when the West Meath Militia from the province of Leinster in Ireland, consisting of 22 officers, 49 NCOs, 14 drummers and 299 other ranks, moved by barge to Scots Flat on their march to Chichester.

The Tipperary Militia from the province of Munster in Ireland, came next, over two days. On 8 June three officers and 375 other ranks, moved from Shorncliffe to Iden Lock on their way to Chichester, followed by four officers and 366 other ranks on the following day. The baggage to be moved on by road from the lock, required the use of no less than twenty waggons. The last major move took place over the two days of 20 and 21 June, when the 512 men of the Waterford Militia under Lt Colonel Richard Keane, passed along the canal to Iden Lock from Shorncliffe on their march from Dover to Portsmouth; 15 waggons were required for the Irishmen's regimental baggage.

Henceforth there seems to have been a commendable effort to reduce costs for operating the canal. Whilst use was encouraged to increase revenue, the operation of a fly-boat washed away the banks and led to an increase in the cost of dredging.

Therefore, it is not surprising that once the invasion threat had ceased, large bodies of troops marched throughout by road without making use of the canal. This made it possible to defer repair of barges and keep the dredging costs down to a minimum. In parallel with this line of thinking, the War Office took the opportunity to reduce the Royal Waggon Train establishment in July to that of a small detachment under Lieutenant Charles Morrison. This consisted of two NCOs, and fourteen other ranks with only 26 horses and one waggon.

On 3 April 1814, Napoleon abdicated and was banished to become sovereign of Elba. Thereafter there was no need for hurried troop movement and so the detachment of the Royal Waggon Train had an easy time, their only task being on 10 June, when Major Robert Lawrence Dundas 1780–1844 together with three other officers and 66 other ranks of the Royal Staff Corps travelled from their depot at Hythe, which had its own small dock, to Scots Flat and on by waggons to Fareham in Hampshire. Next month they returned but travelled throughout in their waggons

July also saw a sergeant and three other ranks together with four horses, of the Royal Waggon Train, being posted to Ham Street where there was a small stable for twelve horses to better the working arrangements for moving the occasional barge along the canal.

Just as summer was passing, the War Office in Horse Guards permitted four men of the 51st (2nd Yorkshire) to pass along the canal from Hythe to Iden on 8 September, with their regimental baggage, and after staying overnight at that point they marched on to Portsmouth with their baggage loaded onto waggons. The main body of the regiment, consisting of 382 men, marched all the way by road. Their move was part of the arrangements for assembling an army to take part in the war with America, which had started in 1812 as a result of privateering activities on both sides. Later Major

Alexander Todd, together with another officer and thirty other ranks of the Royal Staff Corps, travelled by barge from Hythe to Rye on 5 October and then proceeded on by waggon into Portsmouth. From there they went to New Orleans to become involved in a British defeat that in fact took place after the conclusion of Peace, the Treaty having been signed at Ghent on 14 December.

The last part of the Napoleonic saga was still to make its presence felt upon the waters of the canal. Following his defeat at the battle of Waterloo on 18 June 1815, the Allied conference decided to intern him on the island of St Helena. 15 July saw him leave Europe on board *HMS Bellerophon*. With the cessation of hostilities, the Royal Waggon Train benefited from the provision of twenty horses which had become surplus to requirements elsewhere. St Helena did not provide entirely satisfactory facilities for looking after Napoleon, so Lieutenant Basil Jackson, Sergeant David Evan and sixteen other ranks of the Royal Staff Corps, left their depot at Hythe by barge on 2 November for Rye, and afterwards marched on to Havant where they were quartered until the officer commanding at Portsmouth had chartered a ship to convey them to their destination. Jackson had started his career as an Ensign in the 26th (Cameronian) on 11 July 1811 and very shortly afterwards, on 23 October, got himself transferred to the Royal Staff Corps in the same rank. He did not have to wait long before being promoted Lieutenant on 6 May 1813. Further promotion came to him when he purchased a Captain's position in September 1825.

PEACE TIME ACTIVITIES 1816–1842

The canal, thereafter, seems to have become very much a backwater so far as troop movement was concerned, indeed several years were to pass without any real use being made of it. At last, on 29 June 1818, instructions came from Horse Guards for a detachment from the Royal Staff Corps consisting of one officer, one sergeant and twenty other ranks, to move by barge from their barracks at Hythe to the barracks at Winchelsea. They set off on 2 July under Ensign Ernest

Wilford and travelled throughout by water, arriving at their destination the same day and in consequence were unable to claim any marching allowance. Wilford became an Ensign on 2 September 1813 when he was in 35th (Sussex), transferring to the Royal Staff Corps on 26 January 1815. Thereafter he rose to Lieutenant on 14 March 1823 and then to Captain on 19 April 1831.

With the demise of troop conveyance, the need to repair barges which were originally built for that purpose, was greatly reduced, so much so that by 1820 Lt Colonel William Marlay of the Royal Staff Corps was in correspondence with the War Office on the matter.[107]

It seems that half of the fleet was totally unserviceable and the rest in need of some attention. The only other craft owned by the military was the Commissioner's boat and one other small boat, which was repairable. Of the barges, he wrote:

> They are of unwieldy construction and ill-adapted to the purpose of the canal, in which their length would not admit of their being turned and the want of light craft, of easier draft, has been much felt. The prime cost of the above barges was about £200 each, and the price of barges of a lighter and more convenient form would be £90 – £100.[108]

However, two barges needed to be retained for dredging and weed cutting, but the movement of stores three times a week to the various units stationed along the canal could be done by a much smaller craft with consequent saving in horses, (since only a tenth of the space was normally used), After contact with HM Customs at Dover, it was agreed with HM Treasury to purchase from the former the Lugger *Bec* for £43. This vessel was 33' long, 9'11" in beam and 5'2" deep with a carrying capacity of 13 tons. After being demasted, she was put to use on the canal.

The death of the Duke of York, the Commander-in-Chief, on 5 January 1827, heralded the end of the canal's availability for the movement of troops under War Office direct control, for early in the following year the last remaining detachment of the Royal Waggon Train left their barracks at Hythe for service in Portugal. This unit was not always held in high esteem, indeed Frederick C. Cherry, when

30. Coat of Arms of the Board of Ordnance granted in 1801. They controlled the Royal Military Canal from 1837 to 1855.

writing his 'Observations on the Defective State of Army Transport' in January 1825, commented:[109]

It would, however, be dissimulation in me to deny that my mind gradually arrived, by the evidence of facts, at the conclusion, that the Waggon Train is not merely useless, but in reality injurious to the Army; inasmuch as it leads to a belief that a quantity of means for Transport exists, where in reality nothing but useless show exists. I admit that it has occasionally, in appearance, rendered some service, but whatever Transport has been effected by that Corps, a still greater quantity of other Transport has been requisite to supply the wants the Waggon Train has itself created.

Harsh words when one considers that Cherry was Veterinary Surgeon to the Royal Waggon Train depot situated in Mitcham Road, Croydon. His comments no doubt helped towards the unit's end for it was disbanded in 1833. Five of the older soldiers from this unit were transferred to the Royal Staff Corps to look after the draught horses on the canal.

The management of the canal under the auspices of the Royal Staff Corps, was entrusted to Major Edward White, assisted by a lieutenant and a quarter-master, who employed four civilians. The workforce was under the direction of a sergeant-major, assisted by four NCOs, a

bugler and 60 other ranks. The twenty trades of these other ranks, as listed below, give an idea of the spread of jobs that the detachment was capable of undertaking and therefore very little work was ever contracted out to firms in the area:

blacksmith	plumber
bricklayer	sailor
cabinet maker	sawyer
carpenter	shipwright
cooper	slater
harness maker	stone mason
labourer	stone sawyer
miner	tailor
painter	tile cutter
plasterer	wheelwright

In these pre-Crimean days retrenchment was very much the order of the day in so far as the armed forces were concerned, and therefore it was not surprising that on 31 May 1837 an Act was passed for:

Transferring and vesting the Royal Military Canal, Roads, Towing Paths, and the Ramparts and other Works belonging thereto, and all Estates and Property taken and occupied for the same, in the Counties of Kent and Sussex, and also the Rates and Tolls arising therefrom to the Board of Ordnance.[110]

This paved the way for the disbandment of the Royal Staff Corps which ceased to exist as from 30 June 1838.

Two of the privates who were then discharged from the army, had experience of travelling from London by the Grand Junction Canal in one of Messrs Pickford's fly-boats. In the early stages of their canal journey they would have got glimpses of the newfangled *iron horse* belonging to the London and Birmingham Railway which by then had been opened as far as a temporary station at Denbigh Hall, situated about one mile north of the present Bletchley Station adjacent to the Hollyhead Road (Watling Street) just 1½ miles away from the canal at Fenny Stratford. However, before making their canal journey they first had to walk to London, a distance of 65 miles. All 34 year-old Miles Clinton got for his twelve year service as a tailor was a travel warrant for himself, his wife and seven children to travel

TABLE 10: *Analysis of military movement on the Royal Military Canal*

UNIT	1809	1810	1811	1812	1813	1814	1815	1818	TOTAL
Royal Staff Corps (Royal Engineers)	100	56				101	18	22	297
3rd Dragoon Guards (Prince of Wales)			39						39
4th Dragoon Guards (Royal Irish)			108						108
Foot Guards	5								5
3rd Foot (Buffs)				230					230
5th Foot (Northumberland)	2								2
6th Foot (Warwickshire)	2								2
9th Foot (East Norfolk)	69		50	3					122
23rd Foot (Royal Welsh Fusiliers)	2								2
30th Foot (Cambridgeshire)	2								2
31st Foot (Huntingdonshire)			20						20
35th Foot (Sussex)		465							465
36th Foot (Herefordshire)	328	1							329
42nd Foot (Royal Highland)	8								8
50th Foot (WestKent)	296								296
51st Foot (2nd Yorkshire)			50			4			54
52nd Foot (Oxfordshire)	9	770	30						809
60th Foot (Royal American)		20	20						40
71st Foot (Highland)	3		407						410
81st Foot (Loyal North Lancashire)	7								7
82nd Foot (Prince of Wales)	95								95
91st Foot (Princess Louise)	7								7
95th Foot (Rifle Brigade)	528	552	300						1380
Kings German Legion	1427			172					1599
11th Royal Veteran Battalion			112	460					572
Anglesea Militia		135							135
Buckinghamshire Militia	623								623
Caernarvon Militia		124	149						273
3rd Lancashire Militia		796							796
Montgomery Militia	252								252
Radnor Militia	123								123
Shropshire Militia	852								852
Tipperary Militia					748				748
Waterford Militia					512				512
West Heath Militia					384				384
TOTAL	4740	2919	1285	865	1644	105	18	22	11598

firstly to Liverpool by canal and then by steam packet to Dublin. On the other hand, 45 year-old Richard Weston who had spent most of his 27 years service in the Royal Waggon Train, fared a little better, as he and his wife's journey by canal took them straight through to Nottingham, his place of enlistment.

Alas! This opportunity was denied the two sergeants who had been allowed to retain their post of Barrack-Master/Toll-Keeper at Hythe and Iden ever since they became pensioners on 8 November 1823. At Hythe, James Baker with 35 years service, was by then 73 years old, having first enlisted in 1803, when living at Findon, in the Sussex Militia where he quickly got promoted to corporal and then to sergeant. 1805 saw him in the County regiment – 35th Foot – but he only stayed there for one month before transferring to the Royal Staff Corps in the same rank. At the other end of the canal at Iden, William Barnes, with 41 years service, was by then aged 65, having first enlisted in 1797 in the Somerset Fencible cavalry, where after five years he was promoted to corporal. After a stint of two years with the same rank in the 3rd Dragoon Guards he dropped down to become a private in the Royal Staff Corps. His talents must have quickly come to the notice of his officers for within sixteen months he became a sergeant.[111] Before they both walked off home they made an application to the Master General of the Board of Ordnance for a supplementary in addition to their 1/6d per diem. The Board were sympathetic and recommended to HM Treasury that they should be granted an additional £15 per annum. Alas the Treasury scaled it down to £11 per annum, equivalent to approximately 9d per day.

With the demise of the Royal Staff Corps, the Board placed the operation of the canal under the command of Major Ringler Thompson of the Royal Engineers, assisted by twenty other ranks drawn from the Royal Sappers & Miners.

The canal at this period was from time to time used by pleasure craft and even army personnel were not slow in making use of its water for recreation. In October 1841, Ensign Lynedock Douglas of the 71st Regiment of Foot (Highland) came over to England from Canada on leave and brought with him a kayak. Having obtained the Board's permission to use the craft on the canal he came to like the area so much that when he saw the local regiment – 97th (Royal West Kent) – had a vacancy for a Lieutenant, he applied for it and got it.[112]

The presence of the Engineers/Sappers & Miners was to be short-lived, for the Board considered that working on the canal should be the prerogative of pensioners. Eventually, after some vacillation this was agreed, and the maintenance work was put out to contract. This being so, the last soldier left the canal in October 1842.

Table 10 sets out the recorded use of the canal in conveying troops, but even though greater use may actually have been made in peak years, it never really achieved expectations. In case of invasion, however, the canal would have provided a valuable means of moving troops quickly, as well as forming a powerful line of defence.

The excellent two volume work by H.F.B.Wheeler and A.M.Bradley entitled 'Napoleon and the Invasion of England', published in 1908, hardly makes a mention of the canal and none of the 150 caricature drawings refer to it. Presumably the French were aware of it, but the defeat of their fleet at the battle of Trafalgar on 21 October 1805, made any attempt at invasion impracticable and therefore one is left with the conclusion that the idea was a sound one, justifying the considerable cost.

Notes to chapters 1 to 5

CHAPTER ONE

1. Act 33 Geo III c.80 (General)
2. Alan Faulkner 'Grand Junction Canal' 1972
3. Public Records Office W058/1
4. PRO W05/104
5. Ian Beckett 'Call to Arms' 1985
6. *Coventry Mercury* 26 June 1798
7. Public Records Office H050/8
8. PRO W05/104
9. Warwickshire County Records CR1590/1
10. Public Records Office W058/1
11. Warwickshire County Records CR1590/1
12. Public Records Office W058/1
13. PRO W026/38
14. Act 39 Geo III c.20 (General)
15. Public Records Office W05/80
16. Royal Engineer's Library, Chatham File 92
17. Public Records Office W058/9
18. PRO H050/459
19. PRO W058/9
20. PRO W058/11
21. PRO W058/12
22. PRO W012/4640
23. PRO W058/10
24. PRO W058/10
25. PRO W05/81
26. PRO W058/12
27. PRO W058/12

CHAPTER TWO

28. Public Records Office W05/83
29. PRO W012/1954
30. PRO W026/40
31. PRO W058/18
32. PRO W058/17
33. PRO W062/33
34. PRO W040/26
35. PRO W058/19
36. PRO W05/87
37. Ibid
38. Warwick County Records CR1590/368
39. Public Records Office W062/43
40. PRO W062/33
41. PRO W062/46
42. Act:51 Geo III c.106
43. Public Records Office W05/89
44. F.H. Reymond 'Ninth Lancers' 1904
45. Public Records Office W058/51
46. Ibid
47. PRO W062/27
48. PRO W05/112
49. PRO W058/51

CHAPTER THREE

50. Hamilton gives Colonel Jones as in command.
51. Public Records Office (PRO) H0 50/12
52. Grenadier Guards Regimental Orders (GGRO)
53. & passim. Nuneaton Public Library. 'Nuneaton Diary' Ref. LC.942 M.E.H Hamilton gives 'Bristol' instead of 'Liverpool'.
54. Hamilton refers briefly to the events of 24/25 July 1822 as does Major R. Money Barnes in 'The Soldiers of London' 1963
55. The charge of combination was dropped in the magistrate's court, where the indictment was confined to a conspiracy. The combination laws were directed against combinations of masters and workmen; they were repealed two years later in 1824.
56. PRO W017/366 & H0100/206. Mackinnon's Appendix gives 'the Battalion of the Coldstream to march (sic) from London to Liverpool 25 July – 2 August (1823) and embark for Dublin'.
57. Lt Col. Ross-of-Bladensburgh. 'History of the Coldstream Guards.' 1895.
58. PRO W05/90. Also Billinge's *Liverpool Advertiser.*
59. PRO W05/90.
60. Coldstream Guards Letterbook (CGLB), Scots Guards Order Book (SGOB); W017/374.
61. PRO W05/90. Also Charles Hadfield 'The Canals of the East Midlands and London.' 1970. page 144.
62. Grenadier Guards Regimental Orders (GGRO) & PRO W05/90.
63. PRO W03/410 & Townshend Papers in National Army Museum Archives. Ref. 7603-98 Section E. 'The Case of Colonel Leslie Jones'.
64. PRO H041/7.
65. *Liverpool Chronicle* 28 July 1827.
66. *The Warder* 11 August 1827.
67. PRO W017/395.
68. *Aris' Birmingham Gazette* & PRO ZPER31/13
69. PRO W0/17/395.
70. Patterson's 'Description of all the direct and principal roads in England and Wales and Parts of Scotland' 18th. edition edited by E. Mogg. 1826.

71. PRO W05/90 & W012/1742.
72. PRO W012/1625.
73. PRO W0/12/1743-6.
74. PRO W012/1850
75. PRO W012/1745 & CGLB.
76. Paul Vine. 'London's Lost Route to the Sea.' 1965.
77. PRO W03/92 & *The Times* 2 January 1838. Page 5.
78. PRO W012/1745 & CGLB.
79. Wey River Navigation Register. Guildford Museum. ref. 129/3/3.
80. PRO W012/1746

CHAPTER FOUR

81. Public Records Office W047/2646
82. PRO W047/2651
83. PRO W047/2660
84. PRO RAIL1133/149 fol 6
85. PRO W05/117
86. *Military Register* 20 April 1820
87. PRO W012/881
88. J.Train 'History of the Isle of Man' 1845
89. PRO W013/3
90. PRO W012/11205
91. PRO RAIL830/4
92. PRO W012/7942
93. PRO W017/ 409
94. Manchester Central Library F942 7389 M205 Vol III
95. PRO W012/68
96. PRO RAIL1133/50
97. *The Times* 17 February 1832
98. Letter from R.H.G. Thomas
99. PRO W054/336
100. PRO W054/738
101. PRO W047/ 2716
102. PRO W0 52/710–42

CHAPTER FIVE

103. Public Records Office Map MPH 1098 part 2
104. PRO Map MPH 664
105. Ibid
106. PRO W062/33 Returns showing state of canals
107. PRO T1/3502 Treasury purchase of barges papers
108. PRO W044/603 Royal Military Canal file
109. University of Southampton Library, 75–509743
110. 1 VIC c 20, 30 May 1837
111. PRO W044/695(19) Board of Ordnance – special cases papers
112. PRO W012/7878 Muster papers H.L.I.

Regulations for movement by canal, packet boat etc., 1833

ORDNANCE MILITARY CORPS.

REGULATIONS

FOR THE CONVEYANCE OF

OFFICERS, NON-COMMISSIONED OFFICERS,

AND

SOLDIERS ON DUTY, THEIR WIVES AND FAMILIES,

DISCHARGED

SOLDIERS AND THEIR FAMILIES,

AND THE

Families of Soldiers sent to their Homes

UPON THE

EMBARKATION FOR FOREIGN SERVICE,

OR

Decease of their Husbands,

BY

COASTING, STEAM AND CANAL NAVIGATION, AND RAIL ROADS IN GREAT BRITAIN,

AND BY

POST OFFICE PACKETS.

APPROVED BY

THE MASTER GENERAL AND BOARD,

4TH FEBRUARY, 1833. $\frac{S}{363}$

By Authority:
J. HARTNELL, FLEET STREET, LONDON.

PASSAGES

COASTWISE AND INLAND,

AND

CONVEYANCES BY RAIL ROADS.

1. For the removal of Troops, Companies, and large Detachments, from any Ports in *England, Scotland,* and *Ireland,* application must be made to the Board by the Inspector General of Fortifications, or the Deputy Adjutant General of Artillery, in order that due provision may be obtained from the Lords of the Admiralty for their conveyance.

Mode for obtaining Passages Coastwise.

2. When Troops, Companies, or Detachments, Recruiting Parties, Recruits, and the Wives and Families of Soldiers, are required to be conveyed by Canal from *Woolwich* or *London,* Passages are in all cases to be obtained through the Superintendent of Shipping, on application from the Commandant of the Garrison, and the Brigade Major of the Royal Sappers and Miners, specifying the Rank, Names of the several Parties, and the places to which the conveyance may be required. The same principle to be followed for the Passage of small Detachments Coastwise; and for obtaining a conveyance from any other Port in Great Britain, application must be made to the Contractors, or their Agents, by the Officer in charge of the Party.

Canal from Woolwich or London.

See Appendix, No. 100, and Schedule A, Pages 10 to 13.

3. When

4

3. When there is no existing Agreement, Passages are to be obtained at the cheapest rates, and no more than the actual Sums paid, charged to the Public. The Vouchers to be certified by the Adjutant and Commanding Officer of the Corps or Battalion, or the Brigade Major of the Royal Sappers and Miners; and at detached Stations by Commanding Officers of the Royal Artillery, and Royal Engineers. Sea, Canal, Steam, or Rail Road conveyance is always to be resorted to, when the expense is less to the Public than marching the Men by Land. In all cases the claims must be supported by Receipts; and the Officers will be reimbursed (on the production of the Vouchers), by the Paymasters to the Regiment or Corps.

Where there are no Agreements, the actual Sums paid to be charged.

4. Whenever Passages are required from Dublin to the River Thames, except in the cases provided for in Item 1, the Respective Officers at Dublin are to make such arrangements in each instance with the proprietors of Steam Vessels, as may be most beneficial to the Public, the expense of which is to be paid by the Deputy Treasurer in Ireland, on production of the proper Certificates, to shew that the parties were duly provided with Passages, in conformity to the agreements.

Conveyances to be resorted to, and when, Vouchers to be produced.

Passages from Dublin to the Thames to be obtained by the Respective Officers.

The expense to be paid at Dublin.

5. For the removal of Soldiers by Sea or Canal, from one Station to another in Ireland, the Respective Officers at Dublin are to obtain conveyances on the most advantageous terms for the Public: payment to be made as laid down in the preceding Item.

Removal of Soldiers in Ireland to be obtained in like manner.

6. On all occasions of Non-Commissioned Officers and Men moving on duty, and being conveyed Coastwise, or by Canal, Passages shall be allowed for one Woman and her Children to every Eight Men: the expense incurred to be admitted as a charge against the Public, in like manner as that of the Men.

Men moving on duty, the number of Women and Children to be allowed a Passage.

7. If

Soldier will be permitted without the special Authority of the Master General and Board, to embark more than is authorised, viz.—

Colonels, Lieutenant Colonels, and Majors .... 27 cwt.
Captains .... 18 ,,
Subalterns .... 9 ,,
Non-Commissioned Officers and Men for Knapsacks, Arms, &c. and to cover Boxes and Arm Chests, each................ 56 lbs.

and in the event of such permission being granted, it must be distinctly understood, that the additional expense occasioned thereby, must be borne by the Individual; and Commanding Officers will be held responsible that this Regulation is strictly enforced.

11. In all cases where Officers, Non-Commissioned Officers, and Soldiers, are conveyed Coastwise in England, or to and from Scotland or Ireland, and are Victualled at the Public Expense, the usual Stoppage must be made, and credited to the Public in the Paymaster's Accounts, viz.—

From the { Officers .... 3*d* per diem.
{ Non-Commissioned Officers and Men. 6*d*. per do.

12. Every Officer, Non-Commissioned Officer, or other Person in charge of any Party conveyed by Sea, Canal, or Rail Road in Great Britain, is on completion of the Passage to give a Certificate to the Contractors, or their Agents, shewing the number of Persons conveyed to, and from what place; the dates of embarkation, and landing, or the commencement, and termination of the Journey, and that the Baggage belonging to each Individual did not exceed the quantity sanctioned by the Regulations, which Certificates must accompany the Contractors' Claims. Monthly, to the Office of the Surveyor General.

13. Where

Margin notes (page 6):
Baggage to be embarked.
Additional expense must be paid by the Individual.
Stoppage to be made when victualled by the Public.
Certificate to be given to the Contractors or their Agents. See Appendix, No. 108.

5

7. If in Embarking Companies or Detachments, after providing Passages for the Women and Children according to the preceding Item, a fraction of any number of Men, not less than *Four*, should remain; one Woman and her Children in addition thereto, may be permitted to embark, and the expense of the Passage be charged to the Public.

8. In cases of Non-Commissioned Officers and Men, and small Detachments consisting of less than *Eight* Men, being removed from one Station to another by Sea or Canal, and also for Men ordered to Head Quarters for Medical Inspection, and for the removal of Soldiers of the Invalid Artillery and their Families, such charges only for the Passages of their Wives and Children will be allowed, as shall be sanctioned by the Deputy Adjutant General for the Royal Artillery, and by the Brigade Major for the Corps of Royal Sappers and Miners, on their Certificates to that effect, attached to the Monthly Passage Returns; and care must be taken by the several Commanding Officers, that the Returns are transmitted to the Surveyor General's Office, made up in strict conformity with this Item: the expense of the conveyance by Sea, Canal, or Rail Road, of any additional number of Women and Children will not be allowed by the Public, although in the Contracts with the Department stipulations are made for such conveyance, upon more eligible terms than they could provide it, and of which they may avail themselves provided they wish it, and are able to bear the expense.

9. In no case is any charge to be made for the conveyance by Sea or Canal, of Children *under One* or above *the age of Fourteen Years*; nor for the Wives and Families of Soldiers employed as Servants to Officers, unless moving with their Companies.

10. As the Quantity of Baggage to be conveyed by Sea or Canal is restricted in the several Tenders, no Officer or Soldier

Margin notes (page 5):
Mode to be adopted in reference to the fractional number of Men in embarking Passages of Women, &c.
Removal of Men from one Station to another, the Passages for their Wives and Families admissible on Certificates.
Stipulations made in Contracts for the Passage of Women and Children.
Charges, when to be made for Children. Wives and Families of Soldiers as Servants not allowed.
Quantity of Baggage au-

6.

The annexed Schedule A, shewing the Rates to be paid for the removal of Parties and Recruits, the Wives and Families of Soldiers of the Ordnance Military Corps to and from the several Places therein specified, has been drawn out for their guidance; but as the Agreements have only been entered into for a specific period, any Alterations which may be hereafter made will be communicated in General Orders; and these Conveyances are only to be resorted to when Passages cannot be obtained by Post-Office Packets.

SCHEDULE

7.

13. Where Parties go from the River Thames, and embark under the direction of the Superintendent of Shipping, his Order must accompany the claim, together with the Certificate of the Officer or other person in charge, that the Party has been landed at the place of its destination, agreeably to the terms of the agreement, and that the Baggage belonging to each individual did not exceed the quantity sanctioned by the Regulations. A similar document will also be required from the Officer who may direct the conveyance by the Rail Road; and also from the Officer, or other Person in charge, in reference to the other points required to be vouched.

[margin: When Parties embark in the Thames, the Order to be produced as well as a Certificate. See Appendix, No. 109.]

14. These Regulations, as far as may be practicable, are to extend to Men upon their being discharged; their Wives and Children under the Regulations applicable to such cases.

[margin: Regulations to extend to Men discharged.]

15. Monthly Returns of the Names and Stations to and from which all Persons or Parties, conveyed by Sea, Canal, or Rail Road in Great Britain, including Discharged Men, their Wives and Families, are to be made up by the Adjutant, and certified by the Commanding Officer of each Battalion and Corps, and Brigade Major of the Royal Sappers and Miners, and transmitted by them within *three days* after the expiration thereof, to the Chief Clerk under the Surveyor General; in which it must be shewn whether they were conveyed by Contract or otherwise.

[margin: Monthly Returns of Parties conveyed. See Appendix, No. 110. To be sent to the Surveyor General's Office.]

16. The Commanding Officers of Artillery and Royal Engineers in Ireland, to transmit similar Monthly Returns of all Persons or Parties, (distinguishing the Battalions or Corps to which they belong) conveyed in that part of the United Kingdom, in the mode stated in the preceding Item; which Returns are to be forwarded to the Surveyor General's Office within *Ten* days after the expiration of each Month.

[margin: The like Returns for Ireland.]

The

10

Places to and from which the Parties are to be conveyed.	Officers	Officers'		Non-Commissioned Officers and Soldiers.	Their Wives.	Children above 1 and under 14 Years of Age.	Days of	
		Wives	Children above 1 and under 14 Years of Age.				Sailing.	Returning.
By Sailing Vessels.	s. d.	s. d.	s. d.	s. d.	s. d.	s. d.	From London	To London
The Thames and Berwick...	20 0	20 0	10 0	20 0	20 0	10 0	Tuesdays and Fridays	Tuesdays and Fridays
Leith	20 0	20 0	10 0	20 0	20 0	10 0	Sundays and Thursdays	Tuesdays and Fridays
Dundee......	20 0	20 0	10 0	20 0	20 0	10 0	Sundays and Thursdays	Sundays and Thursdays
Aberdeen ...	21 0	21 0	10 6	21 0	21 0	10 6	Wednesdays & Saturdays	Wednesdays & Saturdays
Inverness....	30 0	30 0	15 0	30 0	30 0	15 0	Every Ten	Days
Yarmouth..	15 0	15 0	7 6	15 0	15 0	7 6	Every Saturday for Sunday morning's Tide.	Two Vessels per Week on the average, at times best suited for passing the Bar.
By Steam Vessels.								
Bristol and Dublin......	31 6	31 6	15 9	12 0	6 0	5 0	Wednesdays and Saturdays	Tuesdays and Saturdays
Waterford..	31 6	31 6	15 9	12 0	6 0	5 0		
Cork	31 6	31 6	15 9	12 0	6 0	5 0		
Liverpool and Cork ...	31 6	31 6	16 0	8 0	6 0	*4 0	Saturdays	Wednesdays
Dublin	28 0	28 0	14 0	4 0	2 6	*2 6	Daily	Daily
Dundalk ...	21 0	21 0	10 6	3 6	1 6	*1 6	Three times a Fortnight	Three times a Fortnight
Newry	21 0	21 0	10 6	3 6	1 6	*1 6	Wednesdays	Saturdays
Belfast	28 0	28 0	14 0	4 0	2 6	*2 6	Wednesdays	Saturdays
Waterford..	28 0	28 0	14 0	7 0	5 0	*3 6	Tuesdays	Fridays
Portsmouth and Plymouth	21 0	21 0	Above 14 } 21s. Under 14 Yrs. } 12s.6d. of Age	Under 20 in number } 7s. 20 to 50 ....6s. 50 & upwards 5s.	On the same terms as their Husbands.	Above 14 } 7s. Under 14 Yrs. } 1s. of Age	Tuesdays and Fridays from Portsmouth.	Mondays and Thursdays from Plymouth.

11

Page 3 of these Regulations.

For extra Baggage per Ton.	Names of Contractors or Companies.	Agents at the Out Forts or Towns.	Remarks.
s.			
17		Malcolm Macnaughton, Leith & Berwick Wharf ....London	These Rates include Provisions.
17	London and Leith	William Paulin ....Berwick	
20	Old Shipping	David Gourley ....Leith	The Officers and their Wives and Children to
24	Company.	Mather and Nicholl ....Dundee	have a Cabin Passage.
30		Norman Yule ....Aberdeen ...	
	....	Souter and Ross ....Inverness ...	
....	....	George Barry, Symon's Wharf ...Southwark...	Provisions to be paid for at the rate of 1s. 6d. per Day
		George King ....Norwich......	for each Man and Woman, and half price for Children.
		Daniel Jermyn ....Yarmouth ...	
20	Bristol General Steam Packet Company.	Mr. George Lunell ....Bristol.........	
		Joseph R. Pim...................Dublin	
		John Bogan ....Waterford ...	
		John Lecky ....Cork	
The Baggage Rate varies at each Port, which is seldom charged, but never to exceed 24s. per Ton.	Watson and Pim.	Mr. John Lecky ....Cork	Non-Commissioned Officers and Men to be supplied with 1¼lb. of Bread and ¼lb. of Cheese at 6d. per diem each.— Children half Rations at 3d. each.
		Joseph R. Pim...................Dublin	
		J. Chambers and Co. ....Dundalk......	
		Watson and Reid.....................Newry.........	* No charge to be made for the Passage of Children of Soldiers on duty under 12 Years of Age.
		Hill Charley ....Belfast	
		R. Pope and Co. ....Waterford ...	
40	The Proprietors of the Brunswick Steam Packet, of Plymouth.	Harry Wheeler........................Portsmouth..	
		J. E. Blewett.........................Plymouth ...	
		John Slade, 180. Upper Thames Street ....London	

STATEMENT

12

STATEMENT, *shewing the Places to and from which Officers and Soldiers and their Families, may be conveyed by Canal Boats, and the Terms upon which Passages are provided, under a Contract with Messrs. Pickford & Co.*

Places to and from which the Parties are to be conveyed.	Officers.			Officers' Wives.			Children from 1 to 14 Years of Age.			Non-Commissioned Officers, Men, and Women.		Children above 1 and under 14 Years of Age.		Entire Boats, not exceeding 8 at one time.	Average Time of Passage.
	£	s.	d.	£	s.	d.	£	s.	d.	s.	d.	s.	d.	£	
To or from London and Northampton	2	0	0	2	0	0	1	0	0	8	0	4	0	16	Second Day
Coventry........	2	10	0	2	10	0	1	5	0	10	0	5	0	20	Third Day
Distance from Bromley 3 Miles...... } Lichfield, as far as Bromley .. }	3	0	0	3	0	0	1	10	0	12	0	6	0	24	Third Day
Distance from Stone 7 Miles.......... } Stafford, as far as Stone .... }	3	0	0	3	0	0	1	10	0	12	0	6	0	24	Fourth Day
Distance from Newcastle-under-Line about 4 Miles .... } Stoke on Trent..	3	5	0	3	5	0	1	12	6	12	0	6	0	26	Fourth Day
Distance from Nantwich about 8 Miles } Wheelock Wharf	3	10	0	3	10	0	1	15	0	14	0	7	0	28	Fourth Day
Middlewich Wharf	3	10	0	3	10	0	1	15	0	14	0	7	0	28	Fourth Day
Distance from Northwich about 1 Mile } Wincham Wharf	3	10	0	3	10	0	1	15	0	14	0	7	0	28	Fourth Day
Distance from Preston 14 Miles .... } Chester as far as Preston Brook }	3	10	0	3	10	0	1	15	0	14	0	7	0	28	{ Fourth or Fifth Day
Distance from Warrington about 1 Mile } Stockton Quay ..	3	10	0	3	10	0	1	15	0	14	0	7	0	28	Fifth Day
Manchester	3	10	0	3	10	0	1	15	0	14	0	7	0	28	Fifth Day
Liverpool	4	0	0	4	0	0	2	0	0	16	0	8	0	32	Sixth Day
Macclesfield	4	0	0	4	0	0	2	0	0	16	0	8	0	32	Fourth Day
Nottingham	3	0	0	3	0	0	1	10	0	12	0	6	0	24	Fourth Day
Leicester...	2	10	0	2	10	0	1	5	0	10	0	5	0	20	Third Day
Derby..........	3	0	0	3	0	0	1	10	0	12	0	6	0	24	Fourth Day
Chesterfield	3	15	0	3	15	0	1	17	6	15	0	7	6	30	Fifth Day
Sheffield	3	15	0	3	15	0	1	17	6	15	0	7	6	30	Fifth Day
Warwick	3	0	0	3	0	0	1	10	0	12	0	6	0	24	Third Day
Birmingham	3	0	0	3	0	0	1	10	0	12	0	6	0	24	Third Day
Wolverhampton ..	3	5	0	3	5	0	1	12	6	12	0	6	0	26	Third Day

Conveyance

13

Conveyance per Canal, continued.

Places to and from which the Parties are to be conveyed.	Officers.			Officers'						Non-Commissioned Officers, Men, and Women.		Children above 1 and under 14 Years of Age.		Future Boats, not exceeding 8 at one time.	Average Time of Passage.
				Wives.			Children from 1 to 14 Years of Age.								
	£	s.	d.	£	s.	d.	£	s.	d.	s.	d.	s.	d.	£	
To or from Liverpool and															
Northampton	4	0	0	4	0	0	2	0	0	14	0	7	0	28	Fourth Day
Coventry........	3	5	0	3	5	0	1	12	6	12	0	6	0	24	Third Day
Distance from Bromley 3 Miles...... { Lichfield, as far as Bromley .. }	2	10	0	2	10	0	1	5	0	10	0	5	0	20	Third Day
Distance from Stone 7 Miles.......... { Stafford, as far as Stone .... }	2	10	0	2	10	0	1	5	0	10	0	5	0	20	Third Day
Distance from Newcastle-under-Line about 4 Miles .... } Stoke on Trent..	2	0	0	2	0	0	1	0	0	8	0	4	0	16	Third Day
Distance from Nantwich about 8 Miles } Wheelock Wharf.	2	0	0	2	0	0	1	0	0	8	0	4	0	15	Second Day
Middlewich Wharf.	1	10	0	1	10	0	0	15	0	6	0	3	0	12	Second Day
Distance from Northwich about 1 Mile } Wincham Wharf.	1	10	0	1	10	0	0	15	0	5	0	2	6	10	Second Day
Distance from Preston 14 Miles .... { Chester as far as Preston Brook. }	....			....			....			....		....		..	
Distance from Warrington about 1 Mile } Stockton Quay ..	....			....			....			....		....		..	
Manchester	....			....			....			....		....		..	
London	4	0	0	4	0	0	2	0	0	16	0	8	0	32	Sixth Day
Macclesfield ...	....			....			....			....		....		..	
Nottingham	3	0	0	3	0	0	1	10	0	12	0	6	0	24	Fourth Day
Leicester........	4	0	0	4	0	0	2	0	0	14	0	7	0	28	Fourth Day
Derby..........	3	0	0	3	0	0	1	10	0	12	0	6	0	24	Fourth Day
Chesterfield	....			....			....			....		....		..	
Sheffield........	....			....			....			....		....		..	
Warwick	3	0	0	3	0	0	1	10	0	12	0	6	0	24	Fourth Day
Birmingham	3	0	0	3	0	0	1	10	0	12	0	6	0	24	Fourth Day
Wolverhampton ..	3	0	0	3	0	0	1	10	0	12	0	6	0	24	Third Day

Each

14

Each Officer to be allowed to take with him 4 cwt. of Baggage, and each Non-Commissioned Officer and Private Man 56 lb., the excess above those quantities to be paid for at the rate of 6s. per cwt. but when a whole Boat is engaged no charge is to be made for Baggage.

The Boats are to have a proper security from rain, raised so as to admit a free circulation of air, and to be provided with a sufficient quantity of clean Straw for the accommodation of the Men. The portion of the Boats allotted for the Officers to be separated from the other part by a partition of Wood or Canvas, and to be furnished with a Table and Chairs, or Camp Stools, equal to the number of Officers embarked.

The Troops are to have the use of the Fire-place in the fore part of the Vessel for a reasonable time for the cooking of their Provisions, and the Officer commanding the party is to have the power of making reasonable halts for the comfort of the Men, and purchase of Provisions, but not to exceed one hour and a half each Day.

Margin notes: Rate to be paid for excess of Baggage. — Boats to be secured from rain. Clean Straw to be provided. Accommodation for the Officers. — Accommodation for cooking, and the period for Halts.

CONVEYANCE

15

CONVEYANCE BY POST OFFICE PACKETS.

17. The Postmaster General has consented to the conveyance by Post Office Packets, of—

Commissioned Officers,—

Non-Commissioned Officers and Privates,—

Discharged Soldiers and their Families,—

The Families of Soldiers sent to their Homes on the embarkation or decease of their Husbands,—

On the following terms, viz.—

Commissioned Officers, *at the full Cabin Fares.*

Non-Commissioned and others, *free of all Charge.*

None of whom are to be victualled at the Public expense while on board the Packet. An application for the Passages of the several Persons claiming to be conveyed, signed by the Commanding Officers of the Corps, according to the prescribed Form, is to be delivered to the Agents of the Packets, to whom every possible facility is to be afforded, both at the places of embarkation and disembarkation.

18. The following Statement shews the Stations of the several *Post Office Packets*, from and to which conveyance may be obtained, their fixed time of Sailing, the average period of the Voyage, and the Rates of Passage Money for Officers.

Margin notes: Post Office Packets. — See Appendix, No. III. — Places from and to which Conveyance may be obtained.

Between

Page 17

MARCHING AND PASSAGE

ALLOWANCES,

TO

DISCHARGED SOLDIERS AND THEIR FAMILIES.

Soldiers discharged without a Pension entitled to Marching Allowance.

1. Soldiers discharged in consequence of Reduction, Wounds or Infirmities, or having completed their period of Service, and not recommended for Pension, are entitled to Marching Allowances for themselves; and if their Wives and Children are with them at the place of their discharge, to Travelling Allowances for their Families for the distance by Land, from the place where they receive their discharge, to the Parish or place at which they were originally enlisted.

Rate for the Soldier.

2. The Marching Allowance is to be issued at the rate of *One Shilling and Sixpence* * a day in *Great Britain and Ireland,* reckoning *Ten Miles as a day's march;* and if a fraction should remain on dividing the total number of Miles by Ten, *One* day's Marching Allowance is to be given for such fractional number of Miles. The Family Allowance is to be issued at the following Rates, viz.—

For Family.

	$d.$	
For a Soldier's Wife	$1\frac{1}{2}$	} per mile.
Child (above *One* and not exceeding *Fourteen* Years of Age)	1	}

3. Men

* This Rate is liable to variation, as it depends upon the Rate of Allowance annually sanctioned by Parliament to Innkeepers in England, for diet supplied by them to Soldiers on a March.

B

Page 16

Rates to be paid.

Between what Places.	At what Periods.	Average duration of Voyage.	Rates of Conveyance for Commissioned Officers.
			£ s. d.
Liverpool and Dublin		15 Hours	1 7 6
Holyhead and Dublin		8 "	1 1 0
Milford and Waterford		11 "	1 10 0
Port Patrick and Donaghadee................	Daily	3 "	0 8 0
Weymouth and Jersey		14 "	1 1 0
Guernsey and Jersey		10 "	0 5 0

and care must be taken that in every instance these conveyances be resorted to.

Passage to be paid by Officers.

19. When Commissioned Officers are conveyed by Post Office Packets, the Rates inserted in the above Statement are to be paid by them to the proper Officer of the Packet, and a Receipt obtained, the amount of which will be repaid

Documents required to obtain repayment.

on the Officer's preferring his claim, and transmitting it (duly certified) to the Chief Clerk under the Surveyor General, within *One Month* after the expiration of each Quarter.

MARCHING

18

3. Men who may be placed on the Pension List at a daily rate, *less* than the regulated Marching Allowance, are entitled to the difference between those *two* rates from the place of Enlistment together with the usual Allowances for their Wives and Families.

If the Pension be equal or higher, Allowance for the Family only granted.

4. Men who are granted a Pension at a rate equal to, or higher than the Marching Allowance, are not entitled to any Passage or Marching Allowance for themselves, but they are to receive the same for their Families, as other discharged Soldiers.

Men obtaining free Discharges granted the same as others. Men purchasing Discharges, or discharged with Ignominy, not entitled.

5. Soldiers receiving Free Discharges, with or without Gratuities of Full Pay, are to be paid Marching Money to the place of their Enlistment, for themselves and Families, as other discharged Soldiers; but Men purchasing their Discharges, or Men discharged with Ignominy, are not to receive either for themselves or their Families, any of the Allowances granted by these Regulations; their Pay and Military Allowances ceasing on the dates of their respective Discharges.

Men going to a different Place to which they enlisted.

6. If Men are desirous of going to reside at a place different to that at which they enlisted, they may receive Marching Allowances or Passages thereto, provided the expense does not exceed that of their journey or passage to the place of their Enlistment; but if it should, then they may be paid in aid thereof, an Allowance equivalent to that which would be payable to the place of their Enlistment.

Allowance, how to be regulated.

7. A Soldier who has been discharged, and has received the usual Marching Allowance, and who subsequently re-enters the Service, is entitled only on his *second discharge* to the Allowance to the place of his re-enlistment.

Allowance granted to Men who re-enlist on second discharge.

8. Whenever the expense of providing Passages for the Men and their Families, including the daily Allowance for Victualling, is less than the regulated Marching Allowance by

Cases in which Passages may be granted.

19

by Land, they must be sent by Canal, or Sea, and therefore application is to be made to the Superintendent of Shipping, at Woolwich, who will take the necessary steps to obtain conveyances; but when the Marching Allowance to which individual Men, without Families, are entitled under these Regulations, is less than Passage Money, and Allowance for their Provisions, Passages are not to be found them at the expense of the Public. Separate Pay Lists are to be made for the Marching Allowances for the Men of each Troop, Company, or Detachment, and their signatures are to be annexed thereto opposite to the Sums paid them, otherwise the charges will not be admitted; but in all practicable cases, conveyances by the Post Office Packets are to be resorted to, as specified in the Passage Regulations, Items 17 to 19.

Cases in which they are not to be found.

Pay Lists to be made out for all Allowances. See Appendix, No. 112.

9. For the Period during which the Soldiers and their Families may be necessarily detained at a Port waiting for a Passage, and likewise for the probable period of such Passage, when Rations in kind are not supplied at the Public expense, the following daily rates of Allowances will be granted, viz.—

Allowance where detained for a Passage, or where Rations are not supplied at the Public expense.

	ALLOWANCES.		
	When detained at a Port waiting for a Passage.	In lieu of Rations for the probable period of the Voyage, when not victualled at the Public expense.	
	s. d.	s. d.	
To Soldiers discharged without a Pension	1 0	0 6	Rates.
Wife of a discharged Soldier	0 10	0 6	
Each Child (above *One* and not exceeding *Fourteen* Years of Age)	0 6	0 5	

* These Allowances are not admissible for the Day of Arrival or Embarkation.

10. The Payments of the Allowances while *detained for a Passage* at any of the Out-Ports, and *in lieu of Rations*, will

Payment of the Allowance at Out-Ports.

B 2

21

circumstances, the amount will be charged against their Pensions; and to enable the Surveyor General to check such charges, the Officers above referred to, are to transmit Quarterly Returns to his Office of all Men discharged, whether placed on the Pension List, or otherwise; specifying the places at which they were Enlisted, and those to which they propose to go, as well as the amount of the Marching Allowance paid to them for themselves and Families; shewing also whether Certificates have been furnished them, to proceed any part of the distance by Sea, or Canal.

Quarterly Return to be sent to Surveyor General. See Appendix, No. 114.

REGULATIONS.

20

See Appendix, No. 113.

will be made by the District Paymasters at those Stations at which the Soldiers and their Families may be directed to embark, on proper documents, with which the Men must be furnished at the time of their discharge, by the Commanding Officers of the Battalions and Corps, and the Brigade Major of the Corps of Royal Sappers and Miners.

When provided with Provisions not entitled to any Allowance.

11. When Men and their Families are proceeding to and from Ireland, Berwick, Leith, Aberdeen, &c. and are provided with Provisions at the Public expense, they are not entitled to any daily Allowance.

The Marching and other Allowances to be specified in Discharge, &c.

12. The Marching and other Allowances paid to discharged Soldiers, and the Certificates with which they may be furnished, to entitle them to Passages at the Public expense, are to be specified in their Discharges and Parchment Certificates, and signed by the Soldier.

To be furnished with Certificate of Passage. If not produced within one Month void.

13. All discharged Men and their Families who may be furnished with Certificates for Passages at the Public expense, are required to produce the same to the proper parties within One Month from the date thereof, otherwise they will become void.

Soldiers not proceeding to Places of Enlistment not entitled. For the exception thereto, see Page 18.

14. It must be distinctly understood, that unless Men discharged and placed on the Pension List, proceed to their place of Enlistment, they are neither entitled to a Passage or the Marching Allowance for themselves and their Families, otherwise than under the exception in Item 6, Page 18; and as instances have occurred in which Men have obtained the Allowances to enable them to proceed to Ireland, &c. and it has been subsequently traced that they did not quit the Station at which they were discharged; Commanding Officers of Battalions and Corps of the Royal Artillery, and the Brigade Major of the Royal Sappers and Miners, must apprize the Men at the time of their discharge, that, in all future instances in which they may obtain the Marching Allowance under such circumstances,

Unit moves by canal

1798	June	Buckinghamshire Militia
		Warwickshire Militia
	September	Herefordshire Militia
		West Kent Militia
		Buckinghamshire Militia
		Leicestershire Militia
1803	November	Royal Staff Corps
	December	47th Foot (Loyal North Lancashire)
1804	January	30th Foot (East Lancashire)
	October	42nd Foot (Royal Highland)
	December	92nd Foot (Gordon Highlanders)
1806	December	3rd Foot (East Kent)
		7th Foot (Royal Fusiliers)
		8th Foot (King's)
1809	July	6th Foot (Warwickshire)
	September	37th Foot (North Hampshire)
1814	April	22nd Foot (Cheshire)
	August	47th Foot (Loyal North Lancashire)
	September	34th Foot (Cumberland)
1816	June	Royal Artillery
1817	June	1st Foot (Royal Scots)
		56th Foot (West Essex)
1819	February	Royal Artillery
1820	April	86th Foot (Royal County Down)
	August	9th Light Dragoons (Queens Royal Lancers)
1821	December	Grenadier Guards
1822	April	44th Foot (South Essex)
		71st Foot (Highland Light Infantry)
	May	2nd Veterans Company
	July	Grenadier Guards
	August	Grenadier Guards

1823	July	Coldstream Guards
	August	Grenadier Guards
1824	July	Scots Guards
	August	Coldstream Guards
1825	July	Grenadier Guards
	August	Scots Guards
1826	May	Scots Guards
		Coldstream Guards
1827	July	Coldstream Guards
	August	Grenadier Guards
	September	72nd Foot (Highland)
	October	69th Foot (South Lancashire)
		61st Foot (South Gloucestershire)

Index